RISING UP TO MEET THE CHALLENGES OF LIFE

BRUCE M. WOOD

Scripture quotations in this publication, unless otherwise indicated, are from the Holy Bible, New International Version®, NIV® Copyright © 1973, 1978, 1984, 2011 by Biblica, Inc.® Used by permission. All rights reserved worldwide.

Some Scripture taken from the Revised Standard Version of the Bible, copyright © 1946, 1952, and 1971 the Division of Christian Education of the National Council of the Churches of Christ in the United States of America. Used by permission. All rights reserved.

"Rising Up To Meet The Challenges of Life," by Bruce Wood. ISBN 978-1-62137-583-8 (Softcover) 978-1-62137-584-5 (Hardcover) 978-1-62137-585-2 (Ebook)

Library of Congress Control Number: 2014914874

Published 2014 by Virtualbookworm.com Publishing Inc., P.O. Box 9949, College Station, TX 77842, US. ©2014, Bruce M. Wood. All rights reserved. No part of this publication may be reproduced, stored in a retrieval system, or transmitted in any form or by any means, electronic, mechanical, recording or otherwise, without the prior written permission of Bruce M. Wood.

PRAISE FOR *RISING UP TO MEET THE CHALLENGES OF LIFE*

"Bruce Wood's Rising Up to Meet the Challenges of Life is incredible. It's the result of a life well lived and well led as he truly walked his talk. I continue to be inspired by his life. He is my pastor, and I'm better for his words and friendship. This is a great read."

—Flip Flippen, Founder and President of the Flippen Group; *New York Times* Best Selling Author of *The Flip Side*

"Bruce Wood encourages his readers to "keep on keeping on" by having a personal relationship with Jesus Christ and to "trust in the Word of God" to live the best life possible! Thank you, Bruce, for "living an overcomer's life" and sharing the "life changing principles" that you have learned as you have walked with Jesus in ministry. Read this great book!"

—Judy Graham, Co-Founder and President for Celebration Women's Ministry, Inc.; President, The Confessing Movement Within The United Methodist Church

"The remarkable ability to apply a pragmatic lesson to a doctrinal concept without exhausting its complexity is a unique trait of a master teacher. Christ provides the ultimate example, and author Bruce Wood demonstrates an innate ability to imitate that example.

"With a pastor's tender heart and a wealth of wisdom harvested from decades of ministry, Wood simply and unwittingly presents Christ in a compelling manner that captivates the reader without compromising the integrity of God's Word. In a culture that celebrates distancing itself from the truths of the Bible, Dr. Wood issues a clarion call signaling our essential necessity to know and live the Word.

"If the Bible is our earthly manual for heavenly citizenship, then this book ought to be a required adjunct. Dr. Wood echoes Scripture with a piercing familiarity that beckons the believer to see the Bible for what it is—a book of hope and faith and promises inspired by God to encourage His children to Rise Up and walk in a manner worthy of our calling!"

—Rick Rigsby, Ph. D., Pastor, Motivational Speaker; Author of *Lessons from a Third Grade Dropout*

DEDICATION

This book is dedicated to my family:

To my wife, Connie Sue Plummer Wood, whose steadfast and loyal love has inspired me and sustained me through the trials of life. No other person in my life exhibits more courage, faith, perseverance, and hope to keep rising up to meet the challenges in life. Together, by the grace of God, we have surmounted many obstacles and now enjoy the fruit of being overcomers. Connie lives every day of her life with the words of the Apostle Paul, "Thanks be to God. He gives us the victory through Jesus Christ our Lord."

To our four children, Jason, Jordan, Jennie and Rebekah, who lived the journey with us, and now on their own apply the lessons we taught them to rise up and meet the challenges of life. They are more than conquerors through their faith in Jesus Christ. I fully anticipate with joy that they are passing this faith on as their own legacy to those whose lives they touch, and to our precious grandchildren. They are our victor's crown for running the race all the way through. My heart overflows with contentment and joy.

ACKNOWLEDGEMENTS

First and foremost, I want to thank my wife, Connie, who carried the vision for this work to be published since 2005. She dedicated hundreds of hours to overseeing every detail of the process. She is the silent writer who took the audio recordings and manuscripts of the sermons and turned them into this inspirational book. Your love, support, patience, and vision kept the process alive. Thank you for believing in me, embracing the message, and working hard to make this dream come true.

I am deeply grateful for the excellent editing work done by our friend, Lisa McDonald. With joy she read and reread each chapter, providing quality insights and expert editing to produce a masterpiece. Thank you, Lisa, for catching the vision of this work with a fervent passion for excellence.

The members of Aldersgate UMC provided the opportunity to develop these messages and share them at a difficult season of our lives together. When faced with incredibly hard times, you, Aldersgate UMC, rose up to meet the challenges with faith, confidence, courage, and hope. Thank you for believing in me and for sharing the vision of a healthy, vibrant, contagious church that touches the world with the love and compassion of Jesus Christ. You are my inspiration to keep rising up to meet the challenges - together.

Bruce M. Wood

TABLE OF CONTENTS

Never Lose Faith in the End of the Story 1

Attitude is Everything 12

Change Your Thinking and Change Your World 27

Learn to Expect God's Favor 39

Forgiveness: A Key to Meeting the Challenges of Life 48

Get Passionate with a Purpose 61

It's What's Inside that Counts 70

How to Have Peace in Troubled Times 81

How to Maintain Your Perspective When Life Doesn't Go the Way You Plan 92

Hold On – Until – You Win Out 106

Preparing Ahead for Times of Trouble 118

Works Cited 132

Never Lose Faith in the End of the Story

"Thanks be to God. He gives us the victory through Jesus Christ our Lord." I Corinthians 15:57

The song *I Am a Friend of God* (Phillips, Craig, & Dean 2000) reminds me that a true friend is for you and not against you. A true friend will encourage you to rise up and will not push you down. A true friend will come alongside you, walk with you, encourage you, and help you. A true friend wants you to be blessed and not cursed. A true friend will not say, "I wish you would lose." No, a true friend says, "I want you to win, I want you to excel, I want you to achieve, I want you to accomplish, and I want you to be all that you can be. I am for you – not against you." You have a true friend in God! He wants you to win, to accomplish, and to achieve all that He created you to achieve.

Let's do a listening exercise! Take a writing tool, find something that you can write on, and listen as you read these Bible verses slowly and deliberately out loud. I want you to listen for the word of the Lord to you. What is the Lord saying in these texts? What one word resounds and goes into your spirit? Write it down.

> 55 "Where, O death, is your victory?
> Where, O death, is your sting?"

> 56 The sting of death is sin, and the power of sin is the law. 57 But thanks be to God! He gives us the victory through our Lord Jesus Christ.
>
> 58 Therefore, my dear brothers and sisters, stand firm. Let nothing move you. Always give yourselves fully to the work of the Lord, because you know that your labor in the Lord is not in vain. 1 Corinthians 15:55-58 (NIV)

What one word speaks to you? _____

Romans chapter 8:31-39 is one of my favorite texts:

> 31 What, then, shall we say in response to these things? If God is for us, who can be against us? 32 He who did not spare his own Son, but gave him up for us all — how will he not also, along with him, graciously give us all things? 33 Who will bring any charge against those whom God has chosen? It is God who justifies. 34 Who then is the one who condemns? . . . 35 who shall separate us from the love of Christ? Shall trouble or hardship or persecution or famine or nakedness or danger or sword? . . . 37 No, in all these things we are more than conquerors through him who loved us. 38 For I am convinced that neither death nor life, neither angels nor demons, neither the present nor the future nor any powers, 39 neither height nor depth, nor anything else in all creation, will be able to separate us from the love of God that is in Christ Jesus our Lord.

What word (or words) stands out? _____

1 Corinthians 4: 7-18 says:

> 7 But we have this treasure in jars of clay to show that this all-surpassing power is from God and not from us. 8 We are hard pressed on every side, but not crushed; perplexed, but not in despair; 9 persecuted, but not abandoned; struck down, but not destroyed. 10 We always carry around in our body the death of Jesus, so that the life of Jesus may also be revealed in our body. 11 For we who are alive are always being given over to death for Jesus' sake, so that his life may also be revealed in our mortal body. 12 So then, death is at work in us, but life is at work in you.
> 13 It is written: "I believed; therefore I have spoken." Since we have that same spirit of faith, we also believe and therefore speak 14 because we know that the one who raised the Lord Jesus from the dead will also raise us with Jesus and present us with you to himself. 15 All this is for your benefit, so that the grace that is reaching more and more people may cause thanksgiving to overflow to the glory of God.
> 16 Therefore we do not lose heart. Though outwardly we are wasting away, yet inwardly we are being renewed day by day. 17 For our light and momentary troubles are achieving for us an eternal glory that far outweighs them all. 18 So we fix our eyes not on what is seen, but on what is unseen, since what is seen is temporary, but what is unseen is eternal.

What word (or words) stands out? _____

These texts suggest that God is for us – not against us. I want to encourage you and give you the courage, the strength, the hope, and the skills to rise up from the ashes of defeat, to win victories in your life. I know you would rather be victorious than defeated. As Christians, we often walk around looking like we are supposed to be defeated. No – He doesn't plan for you to be defeated. He plans for you to win!

For certain, there are real challenges in life... there are real struggles in life... there are real obstacles in life. Some of the obstacles are outside of us – some of the obstacles are inside of us. I never want to make light of or lessen the realities of anyone's challenges. Please, hear me! I never want to minimize what someone is going through and say, "Well, just get over it, sister," or "Get over it, brother!" No, it's not that easy, and that's very dis-compassionate. To be compassionate is to take a good, hard look at your reality and encourage you. "You are going to rise up to meet the challenges of your life, and you will not be defeated. You will not be beaten down. You're going to win and not lose." No matter where you are or what challenges you're facing, you can be victorious.

"Victorious" can be defined in a variety of ways. Can the person who has lost a couple of limbs in Iraq be a victorious person? Sure they can! Can the person who is down-and-out, consumed with drug addictions and losses in his or her life, be victorious? Absolutely! Believe it! It is in you to be victorious, and you want to reach for it. You can win! You can change! You can overcome! How do I know you can change... How do I know you can win... How do I know you can overcome?

There are three ways I know of for sure. One way is that the Bible indicates God is for me and not against me. You know these things. It is in God's DNA that He is for you. He wants you to win and not to lose... He wants you to accomplish and achieve... He does not want you to settle for mediocrity. God is for you, not against you! How do I know you can win, overcome, be victorious, and be more than your conquerors? Because God wills it to be so! That's what He wants. That's His desire for your life.

Another way I know He wants you to overcome is that God's word is a roadmap to victory. As you chart your journey to living a victorious life, and you immerse yourself in the principles in the word of God, God will teach you. He will give you principles, strategies, and wisdom in order to win.

I also know because of the witness of others – the testimonies of millions of people who have turned their lives around. Just think about it: You know somebody who has turned their circumstances around by the grace of God. If you made it through one trial, then you know that He's not going to leave you as an orphan to face the next trial alone. He's going to help you all along the pathway of your life. You can overcome horrific and monumental obstacles. You can be happy... you can be fulfilled... you can be positive... you can be hopeful, loving, caring, accomplished, adventuresome, and exciting! Or, you can be a victim – you can be mediocre...you can be bound up... you can be fearful... you can be nervous. You can be defeated... you can be unaccomplished, unpublished, depressed, lonely, bored, and all the rest of those kinds of things. It's your choice.

The difference in overcoming, victorious, and fulfilled life-giving people is that they are possessed. They don't possess a vision; they don't possess a dream. They are possessed by a vision or a dream. They are possessed by a winning attitude – an attitude that says I will win... I will accomplish... I will achieve. I will have a good attitude. I will not quit. I will have confidence in myself and God. These folks believe they can win. They believe they can stand. They believe that if they work hard, they can achieve! They can do all things through Christ, who strengthens them. These are the people who are going to rise up to meet the challenges of this life. That can be you!

I want to keep this thread clear in your mind. I think that a whole lot of what we're asking God to do, God is asking us to do:

> We cry, "Oh God, get me out of financial trouble!"
> He says, "Get up and go to work!"
> We say, "Oh God, heal my marriage."
> God says, "Quit being so mean and ill-tempered. Be kind, generous, and gracious to your spouse."

Think of it this way. We're asking God to do what He wants us to do. That's not to say that God won't help us. He's going to give us a good spirit – He's going to give us a winning attitude. When you know that God is on your side, you can do just about anything.

You may be silently saying to me, "Bruce, that sounds lovely, but you just don't know what I've been through. You don't know what I'm facing. You don't know how hard I've got it." I've got news for you – yes I do! Oh yes, I know. I'm here to tell you that you can rise up to meet the challenges, but you've got to want it, you've got to see it, and you've got to be willing to work for it! You need to begin to say, "I will not allow defeat to defeat me." You need to begin to say, "I will not let obstacles stop me. I will not let trials overwhelm me. I will not let circumstances define me. I'm rising up... I'm getting up... I'm getting out... I'm standing firm... I'm standing tall... I'm going to win. I'm getting out of this mess. I've got the will to survive. With God's help, I will have the victory." God will help you. God will help you see what you can't see. God will help you change what needs to be changed. God will help you do what you need to do, and He will help you for as long as it takes.

Step number one to victorious living – to winning, to achieving, to accomplishing – *Never Lose Faith in the End of the Story*. Remind yourself of this truth every day. This week, tell somebody, "Never lose faith in the end of the story!" Even as you encourage someone else with this thought, it will turn around and encourage your heart. You have to believe that you can achieve.

Visualize with me this story from *Good to Great* by Jim Collins. Jim Collins carefully researched how companies make the leap from being good to becoming great. He concluded that the enemy of great is good. Being good enough – mediocre, getting along, doing fine, being okay – can be the enemy to greatness, to achievement, and to accomplishment. It can stop you from being a person with winning ways.

One of the principals he suggests in the book is that you do have to confront the brutal facts, and yet you must never lose faith in the end of the story. In that chapter, he tells a story about Navy Admiral Jim Stockdale. During the Vietnam War, Jim Stockdale was the highest ranking officer in the Hanoi prisoner of war camp, better known as the Hanoi Hilton. Shot down over Vietnam in 1965 and captured by the North Vietnamese, he was tortured over 20 times during his eight-year imprisonment. He was abused to the point of crippling his physical body. He was tortured unmercifully as a high-ranking official. He had no prisoners' rights, no set release date, no certainty as to whether he would survive to see his family again. He did everything he could to create conditions among the other POWs that would help them survive, to make it to the end. At one point he even beat himself up with his stool and cut himself with a razor to deliberately disfigure himself, so that he could not be videotaped and used as an example of a well-treated prisoner.

He developed and instituted an elaborate tapping matrix system to help the prisoners communicate. You have probably read stories about this, and have heard about it. Tap – Pause – Tap – Tap – and every little tap matrix was an alphabet letter. He's the one who created it, taught it, and communicated it. Even when the Vietcong were getting wise to their system of communication, they learned to use their mops by swishing them on the floor to some rhythm so that they could communicate to each other – communicating hope.

Jim Collins, author of *Good to Great*, interviewed Stockdale and asked this question: How on Earth did you deal with the torture, the pain, the suffering, the violence, the filth, the humiliation? Listen to what he said: "I never lost faith in the end of the story. I never doubted not only that I would get out, but also that I would prevail in the end. I would turn this experience into the defining event of my life, which in retrospect, I would not trade!"

Jim Collins goes on to say, and it's true, "Life is unfair – sometimes to our advantage, and sometimes to our disadvantage. We all experience disappointments in life, crushing events somewhere along the way, setbacks for which there is no relief, losses that are grievous to us. It might be disease, it might be injury, it might be an accident, it might be failure. It might be getting swept away with political shakeups, it might be a turning economy, it might be getting shot down over Vietnam and thrown into a prisoner of war camp for eight years."

What separates people? This was the question that captured Collins' thinking. So Collins asked Stockdale, "What separates the ones that make it to the winner's circle from the ones that don't?"

Stockdale said, "It's not the presence or the absence of difficulty, but how they deal with the inevitable difficulties of life."

The question is, how are you dealing with the inevitable difficulties of life? Are you rising up to meet the challenges, or are you walking around with your head down, feeling crushed, alone, and pitiful? People who are victorious, overcomers, conquerors, and winners are people who never lose faith in the end of the story. Stockdale did go on to say that the ones who didn't win were the optimists. Jim Collins reflected to Stockdale that you would think that the optimists would be the winners. Stockdale noted that the optimists were the ones who always thought the end was near. They would say, "By Christmas we'll be out... by Easter we'll be out... by summer we'll be out!" When Christmas came and Easter came and summer came and their hopes were dashed, they couldn't sustain themselves to the end. See – never lose hope and faith in the end of the story.

What do you need to overcome? What fears do you need to overcome? What do you want to accomplish? What trials are you facing? You can act like a victim and take the attitude that you just can't do anything about it – you just don't know what to do – everything is always happening to you. You can continue to be a victim, or you can pick yourself up by the grace of God and say, "I'm going to win – I'm going to overcome. I'm going to get the victory over this disease, over this ailment, over this attitude, over this depression, over this fear, over my time management, over my lack of accomplishments. I can see that degree. I can see that promotion in my life. I can see my business taking off. I can see my finances stabilizing. I can see myself free from the hurts, the habits and the hang-ups of my life. I can see myself not losing faith in the end of the story!"

God is on your side. He is going to give you creativity. He is going to give you wisdom. He is going to show you the steps that you need to take. He is going to be the stabilizer in your life. He is going to give you courage in your life. You can achieve it... you can win! Commit 1 Corinthians 15:57 to your memory:

> Thanks be to God. He gives us the victory through our Lord Jesus Christ.

Pray this prayer aloud:

Thank you God, that you give me the victory through our Lord Jesus Christ! Father, I thank you that I am a friend of God – that God, you are my encourager, you are my helper, you are my strength. That Lord, you give me the strength to keep running and to keep standing. Oh Lord, you give me the ability to keep learning, to keep growing, to keep pushing. I thank you, God, that I can do more today than I thought I could do. I can go another lap. I can write another letter. I can complete another application. I can ask another person. I can keep going, Lord – I can go further than I ever thought I could, because you're in the grandstands cheering me on. Lord, I pray that you will give me a winning attitude – a winning spirit. Give me a spirit like Joshua and Caleb, who said, "What we see is a fruitful land. What we see is that the Lord is on our side. What we see is that we need to get up and go possess the land." God, I pray that you permeate me with that same spirit, in Jesus' name. Amen

Attitude is Everything

"Thanks be to God. He gives us the victory through Jesus Christ our Lord." I Corinthians 15:57

Friends, life is too short to trudge through it depressed and defeated. No matter what has come against you or what is causing you to slip and fall, no matter who or what is pushing you down, you need to keep getting right back up on the inside! If you will cultivate and practice a positive, hopeful, faith-filled attitude in life, you will be victorious!

There is not a shred of evidence in the Bible that we are to settle for defeat, depression, and being overwhelmed. That is not to say we will not have trouble. Jesus said in John 16:33, "In this life you will have tribulation, but remember this, I have overcome the world." Paul says, "I don't care what you experience in life; you will not be separated from the love of God" (Romans 8:39). He also said, "You are more than conquerors through him who loved you" (Romans 8:37). So, the point is this: No matter how far down you get pushed or kicked, you can get right back up again.

Now, I want to share a story of victory with you. One of our core values at Aldersgate is the importance of community, relationships, and small groups. There is a family at Aldersgate who have been members of this church since 1985. They really did not connect with this church for 20 years, until they got involved with a small group called a "life group." The persistence of the leaders of this life group, Mike and Marcia Lightsey, kept them hosting the group when they didn't feel like going. The going was tough—they couldn't get anybody to come to their life group. They felt like giving up many times, but they persisted in opening their home, and God began to slowly add to their numbers.

Listen to this testimony from these two long-time church members:

> Dear Pastor Bruce,
> Some time ago we were asked to give examples of kindness shown to us. I'd like to share with you what I have received. A little over a year ago, my wife Audrey asked if I would go with her to the life group that met regularly at one of the couples' home. I told Audrey I would go, but I had made up my mind that I was not going to like it, and that I was not going to say anything. At that meeting, I was warmly greeted and allowed to just be there. As the life group ended, Mike, the group leader, asked me to be sure and come back. Something in that invitation made me want to come back, and I'm glad I did. Though I continued not to say much in the group, I was blessed to meet the other six members of the group. After Audrey's parents moved here, they started coming, also.
>
> I continued going to the meetings and enjoying being there, but still not talking very much. Joanne, one of the group members, came up to me after one of the meetings. She said that she was happy that I was there, and that she was looking forward to the day that I would like to talk in the group. I thought about what she said, and it occurred to me that I was

being pretty rude by not speaking, and yet, no one in the group made me feel that way at all. As I continued to go to life group, these people helped me really define my relationship with God, and to learn why it's important to be part of a small group. The closeness of the group gave me the boost I needed for my walk with God. Everyone in the group listened without prejudice to our needs and problems, offered prayer, and advice when needed. In addition to what I was getting from the group, a couple in the group helped our daughter get into nursing school.

Thank you to my life group for everything that they have done. It is rare to meet people that you can truly call friends. God blessed me with all the members of Audrey's life group – that I now call each and every one of them my friend and my family.

Pastor Wood, I don't know if you will read this during the service or not, but if you do, please let JoAnne know that she did help in bringing me out of my shell, but I will be hunting this fall; some things never change.

Daryl

That's what life groups and community are all about—helping us to really connect to each other and to connect with God. The members of our life group come alongside us in our difficulties and help us to develop and maintain a winning attitude. They encourage us and can be our Joshuas and Calebs. Attitude is everything – life is too short to trudge around through it depressed and defeated. No matter what has come against you or what has caused you to slip and fall – no matter who or what is trying to push you down – you need to keep getting back up on the inside. If you will cultivate and practice a positive, hopeful, faith-filled attitude toward life, you will be victorious.

Let me say it over and over again. I'm not saying you won't have problems, but I am saying you can win through your problems. God has more for you than you could possibly imagine. Attitude is everything, isn't it! Winners, overcomers, and victors have a winning attitude. They believe they can win. If you have ever played a team sport, the coach never says, "Look, guys and gals, we know you can't win, but we're here. We're dressed up. We might as well go out and play the game." No way! So why do we say that to ourselves continuously?

People who are winners believe that it's going to get better. They believe they can come back after defeat. They believe that no matter what, all things are possible, and all things work for good. The key to victorious living that meets the challenges of life are the qualities of courage, determination, hope and an attitude – a good attitude, a positive attitude. Folks with a positive attitude always see the glass half-full. People with a negative attitude always see the glass half-empty. Winners believe God has the resources to fill that glass to the top and overflow it.

The Bible is a book of hope and faith and promise; it is not a book of defeat. The resounding note from Paul is, "Thanks be to God. He gives the victory through our Lord Jesus Christ." So, God fully intends for us to be people of hope, determination, promise, and purpose.

I want to take you on a little Bible journey quiz. Can you tell me who these important men are in the Bible?

Shammua – son of Zaccur
Shaphat – son of Hori
Igal – son of Joseph
Palti – son of Raphu
Gaddiel – son of Sodi

Geddi – son of Susi
Ammiel – son of Gemalli
Sethur – son of Michael
Nahbi – son of Vophsi
Geuel – son of Machi

These were very, very, very, very famous men in the Bible. They were the leaders of their clans. They were handpicked for a special mission by Moses. God had promised the nation of Israel a land flowing with milk and honey, a land of freedom and prosperity – a land where they could live and grow and enjoy dignity, health, favor, and order. These men were commissioned by Moses to go, spy out the land, and develop a strategy for occupying the land. Are you getting any clues yet? What are you thinking now? Spies! How many spies were there? 12 tribes – 12 spies! Did the ten that I listed make it into history? Unfortunately, while they did make it into history, we don't remember them as we remember the other two spies. Who are the other spies that we remember? Joshua and Caleb! Read the story in the Old Testament book of Numbers, chapters 13, 14 and 15.

They were given the commission to go in and spy out the land, and to develop a strategy for occupying the land. These ten men, along with two others, Joshua and Caleb, went on their mission. The ten men, the leaders, saw the glass as half-empty. They reported, "Oh, there was water in the glass for sure. The land is flowing with milk and honey. It is just as God said it would be, but you know, it's only half-full – it is almost empty." Joshua and Caleb saw the glass as half-full. The only difference between Joshua and Caleb and these other ten men was attitude.

If you do a deeper study and ask, who were these fathers? They were all fathers who came out of Egypt and brought their sons with them in the great Exodus. They were part of a long tradition of oppression, enslavement, ridicule, and mocking. God gloriously brought them out of the land of oppression, and was leading Israel to the land of promise. They all had the same beginning – the same sets of fathers, the same sets of traditions. But two of these guys, the Bible says, had a different spirit. The majority report and the minority report – the only difference was the internalizing of hope, courage, and faith. Their differing reports reflect different attitudes in themselves toward the land, toward the divine promises, toward the people of Canaan, toward the work involved, and even toward the Lord God Almighty Himself.

Consider the attitudes of both reports. The majority report – ten said no. We can't take the land. The minority report – two said go. Let's take the land! Ten spies misunderstood their mission. Two spies understood their mission. Ten saw God in light of their challenges. Two saw their challenges in light of God. Ten disobeyed God. Two obeyed God. Ten believed that the land had no future for them. Two insisted they should enter and possess the land. Ten displayed cowardice based on fear. Two displayed courage rooted in faith. Ten utterly ignored God in the report. Two felt calm assurance because they trusted in God. Ten suffered from a grasshopper complex. Two rose up to meet the challenge with an attitude of confidence in the Lord. What was the difference? The difference was not in their background, not their baggage, not their culture, and not their past. The difference was in their attitude.

Those ten naysayers spread anxiety throughout Israel's camp; you can read it in the Bible. Their rotten attitude infected the whole congregation until spiritual contagion took over. This resulted in approximately two million people missing out on the Promised Land because of the ten spies' poisonous influence. The whole congregation went back into the wilderness for 40 years and died there. What about Joshua and Caleb? The Bible tells us that Joshua and Caleb stayed alive for a new era to lead the people into the land of promise.

Whose report would you rather believe – the majority report, or the minority report? Isn't it interesting that there is so much power in our attitude, that ten men could persuade a whole generation – a whole nation – to go back to where they came from and miss out on the promises of God? The lesson or the axiom is this: Attitude does make all the difference in the world; attitude is everything. The development of positive attitude is an essential step toward becoming a victorious overcomer, and rising up to meet the challenges of our life.

So, you may be wondering, *Pastor Bruce, how do I cultivate a winning attitude*? I'd like to give you four suggestions. The first suggestion is this – start expecting God to do great things in your life. Listen to Joshua in Numbers 14:9 give his report: "...the land we passed through to spy out is an exceedingly good land. If the Lord delights in us, He will bring us into the land and give it to us." Start expecting God to do great things! We need to start expecting to rise above life's challenges, And program our minds for success. Each day we must choose to live with an attitude that expects good things to happen. Most of us are programmed not to expect anything at all. Many people tend to expect the worst. Have you ever heard someone say, "I can't win for losing?" When my friend, Della, heard a person say that, she yelped, "No, no, no, please stop saying that! You need to start saying, 'I can't lose for winning! The Lord is on my side!'" I asked someone during the week, "Well, how are you doing?" They replied, "I'm here!" I can see that! That's stating the obvious. I'm here, too, aren't I? That's the way we are programmed –to give a negative report.

Listen, friend, you can turn your attitude around. Start saying – today is the first day of the rest of my life! Things are going to get better! God is working on my behalf! I'm going to get well. I'm going to get richer. I'm going to get healthier. You see, it's just as easy to believe the positive report as it is to believe the negative report, isn't it? The chances of getting a better outcome by believing the good report are a whole lot better. We do get what we say. If you say, "I'm barely getting by," well, you will barely get by. If you say, "I just don't know how I'm going to make it," you probably won't. It's in the heart! See, it's in the attitude!

Years ago, Robert Schuller wrote the Possibility Thinker's Creed. It goes like this:

> When faced with a mountain, I will not quit.
> I'll find a way to go over it.
> I'll find a way to go around it.
> I'll find a way to tunnel through it.
> Or, I'll just stay there and turn it into a goldmine.

God wants you to "get your hopes up," but we say to each other all the time, "Don't get your hopes up!" The Bible says to get your hopes up; you can do it! "Thanks be to God. He gives us the victory through our Lord Jesus Christ." Start expecting more. One of the reasons why more people do not come to pray during the prayer time in church is that they've lost hope. They've prayed before without getting what they requested. They've stopped expecting anything when they come to pray – so they are not going to receive an answer. If you quit praying, quit reading, quit trying, quit working, because of life's disappointments, you will not get the help you need to rise up to meet the challenges of your life. These behaviors and attitudes cripple us. So start expecting more when you come to God in prayer. Expecting more will change your attitude and the outcome.

Secondly, stop dwelling on your past. Listen to what the Israelite people said: "If only we had died in the land of Egypt, or if only we had died in the wilderness – would it not be better for us to return to Egypt?" What were they doing? They were dwelling in the past, looking backward. Looking back and saying, "It wasn't all that great, but we can't see a future and a hope here, and the challenges are much too great. We would be better off going back to the wilderness, or worse yet, back to Egypt." As long as you live in the past, you can't embrace the present and the future. Stop living in the past. You can't change the past. There is nothing you can do about the past. Stop blaming the past. If you keep blaming the past, you will keep being a victim.

A victim always blames the past or someone else, and uses that as an excuse for not changing their life now. A victim cannot look forward and make the changes they need to make. A victim doesn't believe they have any options in life. A victim feels powerless to make any difference, and believes they can't change. Listen up – that's not the message of the Bible at all. The message of the Bible is that you can be victorious. You don't have to be a victim. You can win – you don't have to lose. Even if you are born without arms and legs, you can be a winner. You can overcome! Stop using your past as an excuse for not facing your challenges with a winning attitude!

Consider the life of Nick Vujicic...

Nick was born in Melbourne, Australia, with no arms or legs. He had no ability to walk, care for his basic needs, or even embrace those he loved. Throughout his childhood, he dealt with depression and loneliness as well as difficulties with normal, everyday activities. Nick struggled with his purpose in life, but Nick had an incredible spiritual breakthrough when he was a teenager. He came to accept his physical condition and embrace his worth and value, even though he was severely handicapped. He came to believe that God created him with a purpose. With new faith and strength and passion for life, he began traveling around the world, sharing his story with people in stadiums, schools, churches, and wherever God opened the doors.

Today, Nick has accomplished more than most people achieve in a lifetime. He's an avid athlete, painter, musician, actor, and author. He is the president of the international non-profit ministry Life Without Limbs. Nick says, "If God can use a man without arms and legs to be His hands and feet, then He will certainly use any willing heart." If Nick Vujicic can stop living in the past, you can too!

Thirdly, stop complaining against God. Joshua warned the people in Numbers 14:9, "Do not rebel against the Lord." He exhorted them – he pleaded with them – don't turn against the Lord! Complaining against the Lord is spiritual poison. It releases a toxin into your life that utterly sours your attitude and robs you of any hope for victory. What does complaining against the Lord look like? Complaining against the Lord looks like this, if we say it or we even think it: "Why, Lord? Why? Why me? Why are You picking on me? Why, God, are You silent? Why don't You do anything about this, Lord? Where are You, Lord, when I need You? You're there for everybody else, but You're not there for me! I was better off before I became a Christian than I am now!" All of these statements cause me to shudder, because complaining against the Lord is toxic to your faith. It is paralyzing, and it is infectious to the faith of other people. This is what rebellion looks like in His people.

When you complain against the Lord to other people, you are contagious. It is like a signal that says, "Hey, when you are with me, it is okay to talk negatively about the circumstances of your life." They are going to start complaining against the Lord. That's what happened when those ten naysayers complained against the Lord by saying, "We're like grasshoppers. We're going to get killed over there. There is no way we're going to take this land." They infected the whole community with rebellion against the Lord. Keep in mind that what looks like "just stating a fact" can be interpreted by God as lack of faith and rebellion. In their case, they took down a whole lot of people with them – a whole generation had to pass away in the wilderness before God would bring the Joshua and Caleb generation into the Promised Land.

Fourthly, how do we help cultivate a positive attitude? We say of the Lord, "The Lord is with me." That's what Joshua said. "The Lord is with me!" Joshua and Caleb said to the people. They pleaded with them, "Say of the Lord – the Lord is with me!" Who are we talking about when we talk about the Lord? We read about Him in Colossians: He is the firstborn of all creation. He is the creator of all things. All things come from Him, proceed from Him. He is eternal God – He can make all things happen. He's got all the power we need, not just to exist, but to thrive and be victorious in this life. The Lord is with me! Begin reprogramming your mind today. Start believing that with God's help, things are going to change for the better. Not because you deserve it, but simply because God loves you like that.

God wanted Israel to prosper in Canaan. God's plan was not for Israel to perish in the wilderness. God didn't say, "I'm going to bring you out of Egypt and kill you in the wilderness." He didn't say that – that wasn't His plan. "Hey, come follow me, Moses. Take them through the wilderness. Now, you're going to die." That wasn't God's plan. God wanted to get them over, get them through, get them into their destiny. God had a good plan and He loved them. His eye was upon them. He heard their cry, and He made a good plan for them.

Listen – God's made a good plan for you. He doesn't want you to die in the wilderness. God doesn't want you to perish in your self-defeating ways. God doesn't want you to smoke and die of lung cancer. God doesn't want you to live a life of scrounging for what you need. God doesn't want you to live dragged down with depression. God wants you to be victorious. He wants you to win. He wants you to enter into your Promised Land.

Now consider this with me: Maybe you were reared in a negative environment. Maybe everybody around you was negative and critical and depressed and down in the dumps and discouraged. Probably most of us were raised like that. Remember, two out of the twelve spies had a different spirit. They were raised in the same environment, same home life, same community, same ethos. They were all there together in Egypt, but somehow Joshua and Caleb got a different viewpoint of God. Joshua and Caleb were surrounded by negative people. They might have had a "powwow" meeting before they came back to Moses. They probably had a committee meeting before they made the presentation.

You might be a lone voice saying yes, we can do it! So consider this: If you were raised in that depressed, down, discouraged environment, no doubt you're tempted to use your negative upbringing as an excuse to live that way now. Stop using that as an excuse! You can be the person to change your family tree and heritage. If you read that story about Joshua and Caleb, you will discover that they had to suffer for 40 more years. They didn't get to go on over – they got held back. God said everybody who is twenty and under is going into the Promised Land. The rest of you will die in the wilderness except Joshua, Caleb, and Moses. However, the "twenty and under bunch" had to wait and watch for forty years, while each and every person of the "bad report" generation died.

Joshua and Caleb got to bring those little children up, out, and into the Promised Land. Consider being the Joshua and Caleb to break the curse in your family and say, "I will bring my little children with me. We're going to go and possess the land – the good land. "You may have to suffer a while – you probably will – but "thanks be to God. He gives us the victory through our Lord Jesus Christ." You can be the one to break the generational curse. You can raise the bar. You can affect future generations with the attitude and the decisions that you make today. You can rise up and meet the challenges. Desire to develop the *Eye of the Tiger*:

> Rising up back on the street
> Did my time, took my chances
> Went the distance, now I'm back on my feet
> Just a man and his will to survive
> So many times it happens too fast
> You trade your passion for glory
> Don't lose your grip on the dreams of the past
> You must fight just to keep them alive.
>
> Rising up, straight to the top
> Had the guts, got the glory
> Went the distance, now I'm not gonna stop
> Just a man and his will to survive
>
> Chorus:
> It's the eye of the tiger
> It's the thrill of the fight
> Rising up to the challenge of your rival
> And the last known survivor stalks his prey in the night
> And he's watching us all with the eye of the tiger

The question is: What is the Lord asking from any one of us? The Lord is asking us to trade in our sorry, negative, hopeless, critical attitudes for the spirit of Joshua and Caleb – for a spirit that says I wasn't programmed to be defeated. I wasn't programmed to live like this. God didn't plan to bring me out of Egypt to let me die in the wilderness. I'm going to rise up. I'm going to find the grace... I'm going to find the strength... I'm going to find the courage. I'm going to look to God. I'm going to get free... I'm going to get over... I'm going to get through. Things are going to get better. If nothing else, I can change on the inside, even if my outside doesn't change. Circumstances will be better – you will be better! God wants you to believe that He has a good plan for your life – Rising up to meet the challenges of life!

Pray this prayer:

Gracious God – infuse me with a will to thrive. Lord, in whatever circumstances I find myself today, I pray God that You will give me a hope and a future, as Your word says. Lord, I pray that You would release to me the spirit of Joshua and Caleb – the spirit that says: the Lord has a good plan for me – the Lord is on my side – the Lord will help me – the Lord will give me creativity – the Lord will give me a will to work – the Lord will give me wisdom and insight – the Lord will surround me with others who will stand with me. I'm not alone. I'm not going to be defeated. I'm not going to lose – I'm going to win! I'm going to take the land –possess it and go in – and I'm going to enjoy the prosperity and the fruitfulness of what You promised.

God, today I'm trading my sorrows for hope. Today, Lord, I'm trading my fear for courage. I'm trading my unbelief and my negativity for faith. I do want victory – in my marriage, in my finances, in my business, in my work. I want victory over drugs, over sin in my life. I want victory in my life, Lord, and I want the spirit of Joshua and Caleb to rest upon me. Thanks be to God. He gives me the victory through Jesus Christ my Lord – in Jesus' name. Amen

Change Your Thinking and Change Your World

"Thanks be to God. He gives us the victory through Jesus Christ our Lord." I Corinthians 15:57

Philippians 4:8, 9 (NIV)

> 8Finally, brothers, whatever is true, whatever is noble, whatever is right, whatever is pure, whatever is lovely, whatever is admirable—if anything is excellent or praiseworthy—think about such things. 9Whatever you have learned or received or heard from me, or seen in me—put it into practice. And the God of peace will be with you.

God has a mission for you! I'm absolutely certain of that. God created you for a purpose. You have a mission with God 24/7. It's not a vocation that I'm talking about; it's a life purpose. Living with purpose is knowing that you are being called or being sent. God has created each of us for a mission -- to live on a mission, to gain an eternal perspective and align our goals with God. We understand that we came from God, we are created for God and by God, and we are set on the pathway of a life meant to be lived with purpose.

Within this purpose, God is giving us dreams. Simply stated, we are created by God, for God, to point back to God. We are meant to be a trophy of God's grace, so that as we progress through life, others will see our lives and glorify Him. We're God's trophies, and we exist to glorify

God. Got it? You are God's trophy, which is designed to bring honor and glory to God.

Rick Warren did such a great job of helping us understand the life that is purpose driven. He suggests in his book, *The Purpose Driven Life*, that we're created for five purposes. First, we're created to be worshipers of God. In other words, we were created to enjoy God – we delight in God, we love God. Worship isn't simply what you do on Sunday morning from 10:00 to 12:00. Worship is an attitude toward God, where you enjoy God and you honor God and you love God all the days of your life. That's your mission, to delight in Lord.

Secondly, Warren also reminds us that we're called to be a part of God's family, the church. When you're connected to God, you are baptized into the body of Christ, this glorious family, the church. There are all kinds of exhortations about how we're to behave and treat each other in the family of God. The highest is that we're to love the family of God.

Thirdly, he says that we are to bring glory to God by becoming like Christ. God's mission and purpose in our life is that we be transformed into His image and into His likeness.

The fourth purpose he says is that we honor God by serving others. That is, our life exists to serve others. God is giving you breath and life, and He's changed you, and He's equipping you so that you can be of service not only to God, but to others.

The fifth purpose he says is to glorify God by telling others about Him. In other words, witnessing – faith sharing, telling the story, sharing Christ in ways that are relevant, meet needs, and honor Christ as you go through your life. You are created for high adventure living; you are created to live abundantly for the glory of God; and God wants you to run the race and win the victor's crown.

God planned for you to conquer your enemies and march into the city gates victoriously. You were created for victory! "Thanks be to God. He gives us the victory through our Lord Jesus Christ." You are not created to muddle through life. You were not created to be defeated in life – you were created to run the race and to enjoy the fruits of victory. Paul so beautifully talks about the victorious life in 1st Corinthians 9:24: "The runners run the race to get the prize. Everyone runs, but only a few get the prize." He says to the Christians, "But you ought to run the race to win the eternal crown of glory." So, in these troublesome days, I am coming alongside you as a coach and reminding you that you are created for more – you are created for a purpose. God has a purpose for your life. Therefore, get hold of the notion that you were created for victory, and start applying these principles that will lead you to the victorious life God has for you.

What keeps you from achieving your mission or dreams? I would like to suggest the word "encumbrances." Encumbrances are things that are burdensome, useless, or a hindrance – something that is a heavy weight, things that hold us back. Obstacles! What are the things that hold us back? I made a big, categorical list of things that hold me back. There are challenges, hindrances, disappointments, conflicts, disabilities, setbacks, losses, fears, fights, concerns, worries, upsets, sins, shame, guilt – and there is failure. All these things rise up to hold us back from walking in our purpose and destiny.

What I see in myself and in you is that we can't get on with the mission God created us for, because of the encumbrances and the obstacles and the challenges that are defeating us. What God intends for me, for you, and for his glorious church is to triumph over our enemies – to be a church and a people who are walking through this life with a sense of passion, purpose, and destiny. The obstacles and encumbrances are very real, and not just figments of our imaginations. Real or imaginary, they do not have to defeat us. That's the good news! You can rise up to meet the challenges. You can summon the courage and the will to glorify God in spite of them.

We all face obstacles – we all face challenges. But we can rise up with courage and face the giants in life. Remember, you can still pray. You can change, you can get up, you can overcome, you can conquer, you can worship, you can love, you can forgive. You can live honorably. You can do all these things, because God gives you the victory through our Lord Jesus Christ.

My friend Ray is a walking miracle. Ray's son was murdered at the age of 19. Listen to Ray's story...

> Thank God he was a Christian boy. I know that one day I will see him again, but it was a very tragic thing that happened in our lives. The boy who killed my son got off Scott-free. In addition to this tragedy, my wife lived only six years after that; she never got over it. But God saw me through it. If not for the grace of God – if God hadn't touched my heart, I would be sitting in the penitentiary somewhere today. I could take you to the very spot where God delivered me from all that anger – that

bitterness – that hatred that had taken me over so strongly. I hated the person I was becoming.

I was crossing that long bridge going into Cameron, Texas, when I heard the news on the radio that the grand jury had "no billed" the boy that had killed my son. That's when I totally lost it! I was content to let the law handle it, but when this happened, I just totally lost it. You know when you yield yourself to Satan and open the door, he's going to come in and take control. But thank God I didn't stay there. I had friends that were encouraging me to try to get the trial re-opened to send the boy to the pen, but every time I would open the Scripture, God would give me a Scripture that indicated that I should leave it alone, "Vengeance is mine. I will repay" (Romans 12:19). Then, when God delivered me, He put such a love in my heart for this boy that killed my son that I pray for him every day because I wanted to see him in Heaven.

One night at the church when I was kneeling at the altar, God broke through. I would struggle to get over my feelings of hatred and my anger, but then I'd get up and walk out the same way I had come in. This night, the pastor came crawling to me on his hands and knees, took me in his arms, and it felt like he rocked me for hours. I know it was only minutes, but he began to pray for me that the Lord would bring deliverance. And He did – He brought total, complete deliverance for me. I don't know how to explain it really, I was just eaten up with this anger and bitterness and hatred, and as I said, I hated who I was becoming. I couldn't help myself. I would repent, but just feel nothing. When God came in, I felt every bit of that anger, that bitterness, and hatred flow out, and He poured his love into my heart. That's what cleanses us, when God's love flows into our hearts we're cleansed from all of that. When I left the church, I was totally free! I had no more anger, bitterness, and hatred! I walked out totally free and relieved from that.

That's a true story. God changed Ray's heart and changed Ray's mind. Ray is a trophy of God's grace. God does have all the power and all the grace that we'll ever need to live victoriously. Ray could have continued in his bitterness, his anger, and his hatred – it could have taken him to his grave. It could have robbed him of his life of value and meaning and purpose. "But, thanks be to God! He gives us the victory through our Lord Jesus Christ."

You may be going through a difficult spot in your life. You may be saying to yourself, "I just don't know how I'm going to make it." That's when God works best – when we don't know how we're going to make it! Somehow, keep pressing in and keep crying out to God. The key ingredient for Ray was that he kept going to church. He kept praying. Even though God seemed silent – even though many times he left the same way he had come in – there came a moment of breakthrough when Ray's heart was totally transformed.

Change your thinking and change your world! You can't change someone else's thinking. Ray couldn't change the mind of the grand jury. Ray couldn't change the mind of the person who took his son's life. Ray couldn't change anyone else's mind, but God could change Ray's mind. When God changed Ray's mind and heart, Ray's world changed! Change your thinking, change your world. Your world – not the world, but your world! You can't change the world, but God can change your world. That's good news!

The mind is a wonderful gift and a powerful tool from God, isn't it? Think about that the power of the mind for good. With our minds, we can reason, we can plan, we can decide, we can reflect, we can imagine, we can create. We can dream great big dreams with this wonderful gift, the mind. We can think good thoughts. Paul says, "Think on these things..." So when you are tempted to say, "I can't do it!" You need to say instead, "Thanks be to God. He gives me the victory..." I can think on whatever things are good and lovely and pure. I can focus my thinking. I can do it! Paul exhorts us to think on these things – meditate, contemplate, focus on everything that is true and honorable, just and right, pure and pleasing, lovely and admirable, excellent and praiseworthy, and the God of peace will be with you.

Georgia State University professor David Schwartz says this: "Where success is concerned, people are not measured in inches or pounds or college degrees or family background; they are measured by the size of their thinking." Bill McCartney, a famous coach for the University of Colorado and the founder of the Promise Keepers men's movement, understands what it takes to win. Observing this, McCartney says, "Mental is to physical, as four is to one. No matter how gifted athletes may be physically, if they don't have what it takes mentally, they won't succeed." You've got to transform your thinking. John Maxwell, author of many other books as well as, *Thinking for Change*, wrote this: "Unsuccessful people focus their thinking on survival. Average people focus their thinking on maintenance. Successful people focus their thinking on progress." What are you focusing your thinking on – survival, maintenance, or progress?

Paul gives us instruction in Romans 12:1-2 about the renewal of the mind and how to transform our thinking.

> ¹ Therefore, I urge you, brothers and sisters, in view of God's mercy, to offer your bodies as a living sacrifice, holy and pleasing to God—this is your true and proper worship. ² Do not conform to the pattern of this world, but be transformed by the renewing of your mind. Then you will be able to test and approve what God's will is—his good, pleasing and perfect will.

Paul says, "Be renewed in your mind," be transformed in your mind, and he offers three suggestions for doing that in these texts. The first is to offer your bodies as living sacrifices. Translated, that means that we give everything we are to God. Somehow in my own heart of hearts, as much as I understand of myself, I offer myself to God. I am wholly devoted to God. Here's my life – take it, use it, fill it, may Your will be done in my life. We offer ourselves to God. You will never really have that transformed thinking, which is kingdom-level thinking, without first offering yourself as a living sacrifice. Do it now, offer yourself as a living sacrifice to God.

In addition, Paul says, "Do not conform [any longer] to the pattern of this world." There is an elimination process here where we compare the pattern of this world to the pattern of the kingdom of God, and I choose to follow the pattern of the kingdom of God for the rest of my life. I am going to form my life around the values and the principles of the kingdom of God. God is first in my life, and I build my life around God's principles. Paul says, "Be transformed by the renewing of your mind." To be transformed by the renewing of my mind, I practice meditating on the principles and patterns of the kingdom of God. The more I practice meditating on the word of God, the more my thinking will be transformed. Change your thinking and change your world!

Next, Paul says to start asking a different set of questions. This is practical. I tend to ask the wrong questions. My wife Connie and I are proverbially on different pages. For example, when she sees an old house she says, "Wow! Look at that house! Oh, I can see this great, beautiful house." I think, *It's gonna cost me money. It's gonna be hard work. The foundation is flawed and there is so much that is wrong*. She sees the possibilities. So, the questions that have to be formed are – Who can help me accomplish this goal? How can I, or we, do this?

Take this example: Have you ever heard someone say, "How in the world can we do this?" or "How in the world can that happen?" Just changing the voice inflection a bit may change the question dramatically! Say it one way and it leads you to problem solving – but say it with a different inflection, and it leads you to despair. Practice asking the right questions.

Finally, change your thinking by beginning to look for possibilities in every situation. If you are willing to change your thinking, God can and will change your life. Start looking for the possibilities instead of the impossibilities. Change your thinking about what you see – get a God's worldview instead of a man's worldview. A God's worldview is that you view the world and your life from God's perspective, not from your perspective. Everybody has a worldview. What's your worldview? If you approach life from the perspective of: where is God? What's God up to? How can God do this? How can I be involved with what God's doing? Then you are placing God at the center, and you move out from there. Or, you can choose to approach life from the perspective of: Where is God? Is He even aware? Is God even involved or does He care? I'm all alone!" Then you are the center, and everything moves out from you. What is your worldview? Change your thinking – change your world.

Often, we go around thinking thoughts of defeat, failure, lack, and poverty, and yet expect victory and abundance. Jesus said in John 10:10, "The devil comes to steal, kill, and destroy, but I have come that you might have life, abundantly." God wants you to have an abundant life. God wants you to have victory. God want you to be an overcomer. God wants you to wear the victor's crown. God doesn't want you to barely get by in life. God wants to resource your life so that when others see your life, you reflect the glory and honor of God. Go ahead – with the help of God – and see the possibilities in every situation.

This takes me back to the very beginning – the whole point of this is not just so that you can be egotistically puffed up. It is so that you will be a trophy of God's grace. If Ray had stayed in that state of anger and hatred, and he had continued in that state up to now, what would we say of Ray? We would probably say, "Poor Ray, he's lost his faith. Poor Ray, couldn't find the grace of God. Poor Ray is defeated. This thing defeated Ray." But no! Now we say, "Thanks be to God. God is a powerful God, and God changed Ray's life! We give honor and praise to God."

The victory is not just so we can be victorious and be happy and be satisfied and be trouble-free. It is so we can honor God in our lives. Change your thinking – change your world! You can't get to your mission and accomplish your dreams by always being defeated in your mind. God is called El Shaddai, which in the Bible means the God of more than enough. He's not El Cheapo, the God of barely enough. We pray to the Almighty God. We say to God, "I want to be with you. I want to go where you go. Lord, you have all that I need. You've got the supply, and Lord, whatever comes my way by Your grace, I can win. I can overcome. I can be victorious."

You have been through some terrible trials in your life – all those trials can be used for your good. Trials serve as attitude training grounds to shape us into the image of Christ. You can either be defeated in those trials, or you can come out strong with a winning attitude in those trials. Every athlete knows this. If you're defeated, you can lie down and quit, or you can get back up and try again. Keep trying, keep training, keep going until your world is changed. The Apostle Paul confirms this when he says in 1 Corinthians 9:24-27 (NIV):

> 24 Do you not know that in a race all the runners run, but only one gets the prize? Run in such a way as to get the prize.

Park on this for a while: "Run in such a way as to get the prize!" Don't run in such a way as to miss the prize – run to get the prize! God's got a race for you to run – so run it to get the prize. Run with the purpose to win the prize.

²⁵ Everyone who competes in the games goes into strict training. They do it to get a crown that will not last, but we do it to get a crown that will last forever. ²⁶ Therefore I do not run like someone running aimlessly; I do not fight like a boxer beating the air. ²⁷ No, I strike a blow to my body and make it my slave so that after I have preached to others, I myself will not be disqualified for the prize.

What's going to drive your life and your body? Either the body's going to tell you how it's going to be, or the mind is going to tell your body how it's going to be. You start saying to your body, "You're going to have to come into alignment with the mission that God has for me." You start saying to your circumstances, "You're going to have to line up, because I have a mission, and a purpose, and a destiny in life." Change your thinking – change your world! "Thanks be to God. He gives us the victory through our Lord Jesus Christ."

Pray this prayer:

Gracious God, I am delighted in You today. I thank You that You have given me the capacity to imagine, to create, to think, to reason. God, use this wonderful mind that You have given me to direct my life. Lord, I am so tainted by the world that it's hard for me to change my thinking. I get trapped, Lord, into thinking like the world thinks, and I become conformed to the world instead of thinking kingdom thoughts. Help me align my mind and my life with Your purposes for my life. This I pray in the name of Jesus. Amen

Learn to Expect God's Favor

"Thanks be to God. He gives us the victory through Jesus Christ our Lord." I Corinthians 15:57

Romans 8:37-39

> 37 No, in all these things we are more than conquerors through him who loved us. 38 For I am convinced that neither death nor life, neither angels nor demons, neither the present nor the future, nor any powers, 39 neither height nor depth, nor anything else in all creation, will be able to separate us from the love of God that is in Christ Jesus our Lord.

In the verses above, we have the note of victory, of conquering, and of overcoming that is made possible through the grace of God and the resources that He deposits in us. We are meant to live as victors, not as victims. We are meant to overcome, not to be overcome. That is not to say that we don't go through severe trials in our lives. God knows, we go through some very severe trials. We have losses, and hurts, and things that happened, and setbacks that are real. I would not ever want to minimize that for anybody, but the good news is that no matter how far down you go, by the grace of God you can get up! Even though your circumstances might not altogether change, believe me when I say that you can change altogether. That is good news! That is great news!

As you read the following scripture passage, listen for what God is saying to you. What thought stands out to you in Psalm 8:3-5 (Amplified)?:

> 3 When I view your heavens, the work of your fingers, the moon and the stars, which you have ordained *and* established, 4 what is man that you are mindful of him, and the son of man that you care for him? 5 Yet you have made him but a little lower than heavenly beings, and you have crowned him with glory and honor.

What do you hear? What is the confession that David is making? His conclusion is that God has crowned man with glory and honor. At the end of David's great confession of the Lord as shepherd in Psalms 23, he ends with "...surely goodness and mercy will follow me all the days of my life, and I will dwell in the house of the LORD forever." Surely, goodness and mercy will follow me! What is the note of good news in this text? God intends for glory and honor to follow us!

In Matthew 6:31-33, Jesus compares God's care for us with His care for the lilies of the field and the birds of the air. He encourages us not to be worried. He says:

> 31 So do not worry, saying, 'What shall we eat?' or 'What shall we drink?' or 'What shall we wear?' 32 For the pagans run after all these things, and your heavenly Father knows that you need them. 33 But seek first His kingdom and His righteousness, and all these things will be given to you as well. 34 Therefore do not worry about tomorrow, for tomorrow will worry about itself. Each day has enough trouble of its own.

What are you hearing? What are the consequences or results of seeking Him first? What is Jesus saying to those who are listening to His voice? He's saying that your Father is going to provide for you. There is provision for our victory in the economy, the sovereignty, and the care of God. The childhood picture from the Sunday school song is that God does have the whole world in His hands. He's got me in His hands, and He's got you in His hands. When you grasp that realization with your heart and mind, you don't have to worry about tomorrow. God cares for you.

When we learn to expect God's favor, we will live in a new dimension of victory, hope, and success in life. Favor means: "to assist, to promote, to approve, to support, on the side of." When you have "favor" or you are in someone's "good graces," it means you are "special." They will support you, promote you, defend you, and do just about anything for you. Learning to expect God's favor means that we expect God's special help in our lives. It means knowing that God wants to assist us as our Father, and that He is a good, caring, benevolent God who treats all His children with His favor. Unfortunately, that is not always the way we feel about ourselves or about God. For instance, if you have grown up with these kinds of phrases in your heart or your mind, it makes it very difficult to believe that God cares about you:

>Don't get your hopes up!
>Don't expect anything!
>Nothing is handed to us on a silver platter!
>Don't act so high and mighty, like you're someone special!

Can you imagine God saying that to you? There is an element here that you've got to get hold of: your Heavenly Father wants you to know that He loves and cares about you. Without believing that God loves you, it becomes natural to say, "I always get the short end of the stick." That is a debilitating kind of mindset that teaches you not to expect anything good to happen, not to walk with a sense of expectation and favor, and it holds you back from having what God intends for His children to have.

As parents, Connie and I always tried our best to give our children preferential treatment. If we were able, and if it seemed like a wise and good thing for them, we did our best to accommodate them. We gave them preferential time, provision, and blessings. We wanted our children to prosper and grow and flourish and be successful and fulfilled. We were and are always ready to assist them and to give them advantages. We want them to believe and to know that we will help them, always. We want them to live with boldness and confidence, and to expect good things in their lives. Why? Because they are our sons and daughters! Do we expect them to do their part? Absolutely! But we want them to know we will assist them along the way.

Favor is available in the church community for our children because Connie and I have God's favor. Our oldest son, Jason, has been singing all of his life. Around the age of 13, he decided that it was time to begin singing professionally. So, he went to the local sound equipment store and discovered that it would cost him $800 to get the sound system that he needed to begin his musical journey. Being a very hard worker, he mowed and maintained yards in hopes of accumulating enough to purchase his sound equipment. A good friend of ours somehow found out what

Jason was working toward and made this proposition: "If you will maintain my yard, I will match dollar for dollar whatever you make on the other yards." Jason has favor because we have favor. In no time, he had his sound system and went on the road singing.

Favor is a very powerful thing, and hopefully you will get to a place in your life where you know you have favor with God. Because you are a son or a daughter of God, you can experience a new dimension of victory, success, and hope in your life.

To keep balanced, I do not want to presume to suggest that God exists only to be a blessing machine for us. We exist to bless and serve God. He doesn't exist to serve our needs. God our Father delights in giving us good gifts on one hand, and yet if God never blessed us, He would still be a great, good God. That's what makes Him God! So, God doesn't just exist so He can bless us. But He is a Father to us, and as a Father, Creator God, He delights in giving good gifts to His children. This idea of the favor of God is rooted in the character of God, not in your worthiness. You have to get this!

Please understand this: My kids got favor because they were born into my family, not because they were any more special than anyone else's kids. To me, they are the most beautiful children in the world. They are the most talented children in the world. I suspect you feel the same way about your children or nieces or nephews. My granddaughter will be the most beautiful granddaughter that anyone has ever had. That's the way it works. Just as it is rooted in our character and nature, so also is it rooted in the character and nature of God; not in our worthiness or in our having earned something.

When you think about the character of God, the favor of God is rooted in the love and grace of God. Ephesians 2:8 says, "For it is by grace you have been saved, through faith — and this is not from yourselves, it is the gift of God..." The favor of God is rooted in His nature as Creator and Sustainer. He gives good gifts to sustain you in this life. God's favor is rooted in the whole notion of God being our Rescuer or our Savior. He sees your needs, and He comes to meet your needs – to save you and to rescue you. The nature of God is that of a Redeemer, a Healer, a Provider, and a Giver. That's the nature of God. So, let us not get out of balance and say, "God, you're really lucky that You get to bless me." No, God exists because God is God. Because of God and because of who He is, we are blessed that He is our Father.

As God's child, you can live with boldness and confidence, expecting good things. You can expect preferential treatment – not because of who you are, but because of whose you are.

Let me encourage you today to start expecting and declaring God's favor in your life, even if your situation appears bleak. Expect nothing, and you will probably get what you expect. I want to encourage you today to be bold and to declare that you are confident you have God's favor. Start practicing – start declaring God's favor out loud. Every morning before you leave for work, say, *Father, I thank You that I have Your favor. Your favor is opening doors for me and providing opportunities that will bring success. Your favor is causing people to want to help me.*

To be perfectly honest with you, this whole concept of God's favor is a stretch for me. When I was a teenager, I had more favor than the average teen. I was the ultimate popular teen at Lamar Consolidated High School. I was Mr. Lamar,

President of our Junior and Senior class, captain of our football team, Rotary Boy of the Month, Optimist Boy of the Month, and Future Homemakers of America Beau. I was even runner-up for most handsome! Can you believe that? As I have journeyed through life, my confidence has eroded. I have stopped expecting people to want to help me. My self-confidence has taken a big fall. Gradually, my confidence in God's favor has eroded.

So, I decided to try an experiment by declaring God's favor in my life. On June 9, I wrote in my journal, "Thank You, God, that I have Your favor. I have favor with my family. I have favor with my friends. I have favor with the members of my church. Lord, thank you that they want to help me fulfill our purpose and destiny. I declare Your favor in my personal finances and in the corporate finances at Aldersgate."

From that moment, I have been declaring God's favor. Guess what? My attitude is changing. My countenance is lifting. My joy is bubbling up. I have all the confidence I need to move forward with everything that God puts in my heart to do. Why not? God is with me. He will assist me. He will open doors. He will send partners. He will give me energy. He will give me creative ideas. He will give me success! And best of all, I will give Him all the glory! Not only am I changing, but I am seeing God's favor poured out in unusual financial blessings, too. Within weeks I have received unexpected money from known and unknown sources. I think God is demonstrating to me His desire to bless us. Hallelujah!

You can meet all the challenges of life when you learn to expect God's favor. You can experience God's favor even in the most difficult circumstances. When you begin to walk in

God's favor, you become grateful. You begin to see God's love at work in your life. When you begin to believe you have God's favor, you begin to see it everywhere. When you see it everywhere, you get excited! Then, you begin declaring His praises: "Look at God and the wonderful things He has done for me!" Then, you will be able to say not, "Look at me," but "Look what the Lord has done. He has bestowed upon us glory and honor. Even so we take these glorious crowns that He has placed upon us, and we lay our crowns at His feet, giving Him praise and glory."

Every morning before you leave the house, say to your Father something like this, "Father, I thank You that I have Your favor. Your favor is opening doors of opportunity. Your favor is bringing success in my life. Your favor is causing people to want to help me." That doesn't mean that you can sit idly by on the edge of your bed and thank God that it is all coming to you, with no action on your part. No, you've got to get off the edge of the bed and practice the 7 Gets: Get up; Get dressed; Get nourishment; Get to work; Get busy; Get home; and Get some rest. Get favor – never quit, never give up, persevere, be determined to win, and expect God's favor. Do your part, and God will do His part!

I'm convinced that we can all rise up to meet the challenges of life when we learn to expect God's favor even in the most difficult of circumstances. I would like to invite you to make a declaration right now. Say this aloud to God:

> *Father, I believe that I have favor with You today, favor with the people I work with, favor in the decisions that I will make, and favor with the people I love and respect. Thank you, dear Heavenly Father, that You always assist me, always protect*

me, always open doors for me, always cause everything to work for my good. Today I boldly proclaim Your favor, and I gladly give You all the honor and the glory. Amen.

What would happen in your life if you carried this around and read it so often that you got it into your spirit – not as just a momentary thing you did today, but as an attitude, as a faith position reflecting the confidence and boldness you have in God? I think it could revolutionize your life.

The most significant place to begin to tap into God favor is to truly become God's son or daughter. The Bible declares, "to all who received Him, to those who believed in His name, He gave the right to become children of God – children born not of natural descent, not of human decision or a husband's will, but from God." (John 1:12-13). God loves you. He desires to have a relationship with you. He wants you to know Him, and He wants you to have a life filled with purpose and victory. When you put your trust and hope in Jesus Christ, you can really begin to have mastery in life and an eternal home when you die. Today I urge you, if you have never turned your life over to Jesus Christ, to pray this prayer right now...

"Heavenly Father, I thank You that You are the awesome and great God who desires for me to live life in Your favor. Here and now, I surrender my life to You. Take my life. I want to be a child of God. I believe that Jesus Christ died for me, and I believe that He lives. I promise that, by the mercy and help of God, I will honor You in all my life. I will gladly tell of Your great love – In Jesus' name. Amen."

Forgiveness: A Key to Meeting the Challenges of Life

"Thanks be to God. He gives us the victory through Jesus Christ our Lord." I Corinthians 15:57

A churchgoer wrote a letter to the editor of the newspaper and complained that it made no sense to go to church every Sunday. He wrote:

> I've gone to church for thirty years now, and in that time I've heard something like 3,000 sermons, but for the life of me, I can't remember a single one of them. So, I'm thinking that it's a waste of my time and a waste of the preacher's time, too.

This started a real controversy in the letters to the editor, much to the delight of the editor. This went on for weeks, until someone wrote this clincher:

> I been married for thirty years now, and in that time my wife has cooked something like thirty-two thousand meals, but for the life of me, I can't remember one entire menu of one single meal in all those years. However, I do know this: that they all nourished me and gave me the strength I needed to do my work. If my wife had not given me these meals, I would be physically dead today! Likewise, if I had not gone to church for nourishment, I would be spiritually dead today!

When you are down to nothing, God is up to something! Faith sees the invisible, believes the incredible, and receives the impossible. Thank God for our physical and spiritual nourishment. Keep coming to church. You won't remember a thing that I said (sometimes I don't remember myself!), but it will nourish you (I am sure of that!) because the word of God never returns void. The word of God always accomplishes its purpose in our minds and in our hearts. I am thankful for the word of God.

Take a look at Matthew 18:23-35 (NIV) about the story of the unforgiving debtor:

> 23 "Therefore, the kingdom of heaven is like a king who wanted to settle accounts with his servants. 24 As he began the settlement, a man who owed him ten thousand bags of gold was brought to him. 25 Since he was not able to pay, the master ordered that he and his wife and his children and all that he had be sold to repay the debt.
> 26 "At this the servant fell on his knees before him. 'Be patient with me,' he begged, 'and I will pay back everything.' 27 The servant's master took pity on him, canceled the debt and let him go.
> 28 "But when that servant went out, he found one of his fellow servants who owed him a hundred silver coins. He grabbed him and began to choke him. 'Pay back what you owe me!' he demanded.
> 29 "His fellow servant fell to his knees and begged him, 'Be patient with me, and I will pay it back.'
> 30 "But he refused. Instead, he went off and had the man thrown into prison until he could pay the debt. 31 When the other servants saw what had happened, they were outraged and went and told their master everything that had happened.

32 "Then the master called the servant in. 'You wicked servant,' he said, 'I canceled all that debt of yours because you begged me to. **33** Shouldn't you have had mercy on your fellow servant just as I had on you?' **34** In anger his master handed him over to the jailers to be tortured, until he should pay back all he owed.

35 "This is how my heavenly Father will treat each of you unless you forgive your brother or sister from your heart."

The lesson is crystal clear to me. To begin with, God in His mercy forgives us our great debt. That point is obvious in the story, isn't it? The king had a servant indebted to him, and the king forgave the servant's great debt. Secondly, when we are forgiven, we are to forgive those indebted to us. Isn't that right? Thirdly, if we do not forgive our debtors, if we refuse to forgive as we were forgiven, we will be in bondage until we pay back all that we owe.

It's a simple story, but profound in its application. We have been forgiven much; what right do we have to hold others in bondage for the little they owe us? If we refuse to forgive, we ourselves will end up in a prison of our own making.

Nothing is more needful or practical about living the Christian life than dealing with conflict in the human spirit. Have you had conflict with another human in your life, either with roommates (the joy and the pain), husbands or wives (Oh! the joy and the pain), family members, or church staff?

I got an invitation to attend the retirement celebration of the church secretary who worked for me and with me a number of years ago. She served for 20 years in a couple of church offices, and I thought, if I go to that retirement party I'm going to say:

> Dorothea is a saint, because after 19 years of working inside the church for all of those pastors, and with all of those lay-people, she still loves God and still loves the church. It's a miracle!

Even in the church, there are painful and disappointing relationships. All of us can relate one way or the other. We all know the hurt, the frustration, and the disappointment of discord, betrayal, or broken relationships. Is there a route, a way to find healing when we have broken relationships? Is there a way to live the Christian life so that we live in love and forgiveness? There must be, or there wouldn't be stories like this in the Bible. Neither would there be the exhortations in the Scripture that encourage us to forgive.

On forgiveness, Jesus said, in Matthew 6:9-13, 9 "This, then, is how you should pray:

> 'Our Father in heaven, hallowed be your name,
> [10] your kingdom come, your will be done,
> On earth as it is in heaven.
> [11] Give us today our daily bread.
> [12] **And forgive us our debts,**
> **as we also have forgiven our debtors.**
> [13] And lead us not into temptation,
> but deliver us from the evil one.'
> [14] For if you forgive other people when they sin against you, your heavenly Father will also forgive you. [15] But if you do not forgive others their sins, your Father will not forgive your sins."

Jesus is saying, here is the pattern that you pray every time you pray. Ask the Lord to forgive your debts, and to give you the grace to forgive your debtors. Have you ever had anyone owe you a large debt? Have you ever owed a debt that you thought you couldn't pay? Paul exhorts the church to "be kind to one another, tenderhearted, forgiving one another, as God in Christ forgave you" (Ephesians 4:32).

There are three concerns when talking about forgiveness: 1) what forgiveness is not; 2) why should we forgive; and 3) how we can forgive from the heart. Remember what Jesus said: "My father will do to you what he did to that servant if you do not forgive from your heart" (Matthew 18:35).

To begin with, consider what forgiveness is not. Forgiveness is not forgetting. Get that clear in your mind. Forgiveness is not forgetting. It is an American colloquialism to say, *"Oh, forgive and forget!"* Do you have trouble forgiving and forgetting? Of course you do! Your brain isn't wired that way. The brain has a unique ability to remember and store information. You don't forget experiences in your life, unless you go through traumatic stress syndrome. Traumatic Stress Syndrome is the capacity of the mind, when you are terribly traumatized or shocked, to erase the memory of that experience to avoid the pain. Nonetheless, most of us can remember the offense with clarity. Forgiveness is not forgetting; forgiveness is letting go. When you really experience forgiveness in your life, you will be able to remember the experience, even talk about the experience in a sane manner, and say, *wasn't that terrible, but thank God, I'm forgiven. I'm not in prison anymore!* So, forgiveness is not forgetting.

Neither is forgiveness ignoring what's happened. It is not just "sweeping it under the rug." It is not just forgetting it or denying it. It is not ignoring it or excusing it. If we deny it, or overlook it, or excuse it, the chances are pretty high that it's going to come back to haunt us, and we're going to end up in bondage or imprisoned anyway. We are better off not to deny it, but to look at it and deal with it.

Why should we forgive? Here are four reasons from the Bible why we should forgive. First, we should forgive because God commands it. You can get around it all you want to, you can justify yourself as much as you'd like to, but obedience requires that we walk in forgiveness. The Bible says, "...be kind to one another, tenderhearted, forgiving each other" and "forgive us our debts as we forgive our debtors." In the story, you have the king who forgives the debtor and the debtor who turns around and holds his servant indebted to him. God commands it – forgive!

Secondly, we forgive because God has forgiven us! Have you been forgiven? Jesus explains to His disciples the correlation between forgiveness and love in Luke 7 (NIV) when He explains why He allowed a sinful woman to pour oil over His feet and wipe His feet with her hair (she shouldn't have been touching Him, according to the Law):

> 47 Therefore, I tell you, her many sins have been forgiven—as her great love has shown. But whoever has been forgiven little loves little.

Jesus explains that the person with great sin receives great forgiveness, and in turn demonstrates great love to God. Those who have been forgiven much love much.

The idea here is that we forgive others because God has forgiven us. In 2Corinthians 5:21, Paul says:

> 21 God made him who had no sin to be sin for us, so that in him we might become the righteousness of God.

God has forgiven us a great debt. Too often we forget that! We forget that He died on the cross, He was nailed to a tree, and He gave His life freely for our forgiveness. The whole point of the cross is sin and forgiveness and liberation. Having been forgiven a great debt, we are to forgive others.

The third reason we forgive is because our very own freedom depends on it. Again, your freedom depends on it! Unforgiveness leads to bondage. Ultimately, forgiveness is not about the other person, it's about liberating yourself from your own bondage. If you don't let offenders off the hook, you stay hooked to them. If you stay hooked to them, the past stays with you. That means you have continued pain in your life. It just makes sense to let it go. It is like having a poison in your body and inviting that poison to remain in your body. You will continue to be sick all your life, even though you have an antidote to get the poison out of your body. It is called forgiveness! The ramifications of unforgiveness are legion. Imagine that you have been arrested and taken to prison. In your hand are the keys to unlock your cell, release you, and set you free. You hold the keys to your own freedom.

Once I was put in the county jail as a fundraiser for some organization. I had to raise $300 by calling my friends to donate to the cause and get me out of jail. Being a pastor was an advantage to me, because I called the church administrator, Patsy, and asked her to bring me the church directory. I found out who my friends were really quickly.

Have you gotten this mental picture of a person in jail, holding in their hand the keys to their own freedom? That's what unforgiveness does. It is bondage and it puts you in jail. Unforgiveness actually makes you a prisoner controlled by a sinful nature. Romans 6:23 in the Bible says whoever is controlled by his sinful nature is death. If you're controlled by a sinful nature, you are in prison. You are perpetuating a living death. Examples of a sinful nature are: anger, retaliation, silence, rage, rejection, harshness, criticism. You become a person that is cynical, and even a person who slanders. So you see, forgiveness just makes sense (doesn't it?) if you want to live free.

The fourth reason to forgive is because forgiveness is a means of grace in the offender's life. How else will people know about the love of God, unless they learn it through people gifted with God's grace who extend the mercy of God to them?

Think about how the story would have been different in Matthew 18 if the king had said that he wanted to settle all his accounts, then he pulled the servant in and said, "You, your wife, and your children will stay in prison until the debt is paid." In horror at the consequences, the servant pleads with the king, "Oh, please forgive my debt. I will repay." The king forgives his debts, and the rejoicing servant goes to the one who owes him — and instead of collecting his debt, the servant forgives him and says, "Look, brother, I know you owe me, but I've been forgiven so much that I'm going to release you from what you owe me. I forgive you." What a different story this would have been. If we applied this "pay it forward" attitude to our lives, what a different story this would be in our relationships. What a difference it makes in your life when you forgive as God has forgiven you! What freedom from bondage and stress this would produce!

The third question is: How can I forgive from the heart? There are six keys for forgiving from the heart. Key number one is to admit to God how you feel regarding the offense that happened in your life. That's moving out of denial, looking at it face-to-face, and admitting that this really hurts. This means being able to admit to God that you have this hurt in your life that has you in a prison, and you can't let it go. You can't forgive. In your mind and heart you feel that the offender has crossed the line. You wonder how God can expect you to forgive after what they have done. Tell God the truth about what you feel. Admit it to God.

When you're working on forgiveness, I suggest four lists. Take a piece of paper and draw four columns with these headings: 1) the first column is what the person did or didn't do to you; 2) the second column is all the hurts that you felt; 3) the third is the ramifications of the offense, and 4) the fourth column is your sinful reactions to the hurt.

Fill in the first column — write down what the person did, or didn't do. People will hurt us not only through what they do, but through what they don't do. Sometimes what they don't do hurts us just as much as what they do. They didn't love me, they didn't forgive me, they didn't notice me, they didn't remember our anniversary, or they weren't there for me. It was what they didn't do that caused pain and brought about unforgiveness. Make a list of those things: I was abused, I was abandoned and betrayed, I was deceived, or I was lied to. Has this happened to you? You know it has happened to you, and it hurt when that happened.

Once you've completed the first column, move to the second column. What was the emotion of that hurt? Fill in the second column. Most of us are not good with emotion words, particularly men. For example, our son Jordan would come home from school and we'd quiz him about his day. We'd invariably ask, "How do you feel about that, Jordan?" He would reply, "Good!" Good was his stock response to questions about his feelings. He has now expanded his emotional repertoire to, "I feel great." Most of us only identify a couple of feeling words. One is anger, and another is sadness. I feel really angry. I feel really sad. There are a whole host of feeling words that we need to identify, such as: I felt belittled, I felt defiled, I felt alone, I felt cheated, I felt ridiculed, I felt rejected; it hurt when that happened in my life.

After completing column two, fill in the third column with the ramifications of the offense. There are some long-term ramifications that happen in our lives as a result of being hurt by others, and there is unforgiveness. For instance, we make sweeping conclusions such as "no men are to be trusted." As I listen, I think to myself, *I know there a lot of crummy men, but aren't there a few good men out there?* Another example is "I will never give my heart fully to another person." With this thinking, we guard ourselves, and when we guard ourselves, we put ourselves in prison. What we believe is protection becomes our bondage. What are the ramifications as a result of the hurt in your own life?

The fourth column (which I know you will love to fill out) is your sinful reactions. Do you know that you have some responsibility to bear in unforgiveness? Somebody did something to hurt you, but I can guarantee you didn't react out of love. The sinful nature took over, and you reacted according to the flesh. What are some those reactions? One reaction is bitterness — the very mention of their name brings up a flare in you. Another reaction is gossip — we can't wait to let someone know what they did to us. Take a look at punishment — oh my Lord, we punish people! We punish to gain control of them and the situation. If you have ever experienced the silent treatment, you have experienced punishment. If you have given the silent treatment, you know how it works. You may know of family members that haven't talked to each other in 10 years or more. Who are they punishing, really? Who is in prison? Examples of other sinful reactions are: rejection, resentment, anger, revenge, and the like.

So, let's review. The first key is to make a list, and admit to God and to yourself how you felt regarding the offense. The second key is to decide to extend forgiveness to the person who has hurt you. Don't wait until you feel like forgiving. You may never feel like it. Exercise the will that God has given you. You don't wait until you feel like forgiving. Feelings take time to heal after the choice to forgive has been made. God is your helper and your strength. If the word of God says that you can do it, then you can do it! Don't say, "God, I want to forgive, but..." Make this declaration: "In the name of Jesus, I forgive _____ for _____!" You decide, and then you act. Then, the grace of God will work to heal the hurt that is in your heart.

The third key is: Put the offender in God's hands and let it go! Remember, you are not God. The sooner you get that, the happier you will be. The Bible says in Romans 12:19:

> Do not take revenge, my dear friends, but leave room for God's wrath, for it is written: "It is mine to avenge; I will repay," says the Lord.

See, now you are taking your hands off and letting go. You're not in charge of their judgment. You're not in charge of their condemnation. You're not in charge of what God wants to do with them. God is in charge of them, and all you have to give them to God. Put them in God's hands.

Key number four is: Name and confess (confession is simply agreeing with God). For instance, God says that I'm a sinner, and I agree. Confess to God that your simple reactions and attitudes are wrong. Remember, 1 John 1:9 (NIV) says, "9 If we confess our sins, he is faithful and just and will forgive us our sins and purify us from all unrighteousness." Be glad for that! We all have some work to do in this area of our lives.

Key number five is: Choose to live like the new creation that you are. First Corinthians 5:17 says, "Behold, all things are new." You are a new creation in Christ! If you are a new creation, then act like it! We say in our family: *fake it until you make it!* Meanwhile, until it is real to you, ask the Lord for His help. Declare, "I am a new creation in Christ. I've been made new. I have a renewed mind. I need to act like it." Faith works! Lay aside those fleshly reactions.

The sixth key is: You are willing to be reconciled to the offender, and to allow God to love the offender through you. *Good grief! I didn't know we had to do that.* Tell God, "I'm willing to be reconciled to the offender," and at that point simply say, "You know what, God, I can't, but You can. You are going to have to do this through me." Forgiveness is a lifestyle that takes the sanctifying grace of God to be made perfect in Him.

Here is a bit of practical advice for you. Have you ever had someone come and confess that you were the one who had hurt them, and that they had forgiven you? Imagine that person saying, "Sister or Brother, I just want you to know that I forgive you." Doing that is not necessary, and you have just made the other person angry. Now, I will be aware that you don't like me. Revealing your unforgiveness is not necessary. This is a God thing, between you and God. When

God heals your heart, you are able to let it go and walk in forgiveness. You start walking as a reconciled, born-again, loving person, and start blessing the offender in the name of the Lord. It won't take very long for them to know that you have forgiven them.

Your will needs to cooperate with the Spirit Who is nudging you to get things right. Don't stay in prison holding unforgiveness toward your mama, your daddy, your brother, your sister, your aunt, your uncle, your coworker who cheated you, your coworker who lied, or your roommate who took your deposit and didn't pay it back. Set yourself free! That is the hope. Pray this prayer:

Gracious God, I am reminded of Your mercies that are new every morning – forgiveness. I am like the man in the story who was deeply indebted to You. You forgave my debts, as great as they were. Lord, I have to confess that as a forgiven person, I turned around and said to those who offended me, 'I will not forgive.' I have imprisoned myself, O Lord. I pray that You will break the chain and remove the bars that hold me in bondage. I have become critical, cynical, harsh, I've spoken ill, and I have gossiped about my offenders. It is not becoming to You, Lord. It is not becoming to me. God, I want to be free. So, Lord, I surrender to You. Do a work in me. I pray this in the name of Jesus. Amen.

Get Passionate with a Purpose

"Thanks be to God. He gives us the victory through Jesus Christ our Lord." I Corinthians 15:57

In the journey to acquire the skills to rise up and meet the challenges of life, it is important to learn to listen to God. Open your heart. Listen for God's word to you. God's word to you might be different than God's word to me. There is the general written word of God, but it's amazing how God can take that word and speak personally to you and me. So, while you are reading this, listen for God's word to you. What stands out in your mind? When you focus on that special word God has given you in the Bible, you can make it through the rest of the week – you can rise up to meet any challenge that you face.

The passage below is found in 2 Corinthians 4:7-18. Listen to Paul's heart as he writes to the church in Corinth:

> 7 But we have this treasure in jars of clay to show that this all-surpassing power is from God and not from us. 8 We are hard pressed on every side, but not crushed; perplexed, but not in despair; 9 persecuted, but not abandoned; struck down, but not destroyed. 10 We always carry around in our body the death of Jesus, so that the life of Jesus may also be revealed in our body. 11 For we who are alive are always being given over to death for Jesus' sake, so that his life may also be revealed in our mortal body. 12 So then, death is at work in us, but life is at work in you.

13 It is written: "I believed; therefore I have spoken." Since we have that same spirit of faith, we also believe and therefore speak, **14** because we know that the one who raised the Lord Jesus from the dead will also raise us with Jesus and present us with you to himself. **15** All this is for your benefit, so that the grace that is reaching more and more people may cause thanksgiving to overflow to the glory of God.

16 Therefore we do not lose heart. Though outwardly we are wasting away, yet inwardly we are being renewed day by day. **17** For our light and momentary troubles are achieving for us an eternal glory that far outweighs them all. **18** So we fix our eyes not on what is seen, but on what is unseen, since what is seen is temporary, but what is unseen is eternal.

I would like for you to consider our witness – Connie's and my witness – and the way that we identify with Paul in both his suffering and confidence in the Lord. Not long ago, Connie and I were making a short trip from College Station to Huntsville, taking Highway 30 – a beautiful drive. It was early in the morning and, along the way we went through the little town of Shiro, Texas. Shiro was once a thriving community; now, it is almost a ghost town. As we came into Shiro, our hearts and minds were flooded with memories of the days we spent there. For you see, we pastored Shiro United Methodist Church in Shiro, Texas, from 1973 to 1976. We decided to pause and take a little detour down an overgrown dirt lane, and we parked in front of the picturesque white wood-framed church. Not much had changed in 30 years, with its little steeple and manicured lawn. It was reminiscent of the song *Church in the Wildwood* (Pitts & Owen).

> Come to the church by the Wildwood
> Oh, come to the church in the vale
> No spot is so dear to my childhood
> As the little brown (white) church in the vale

We got out of our car, went to the double front doors, and jiggled the door handle. It was locked, so we sat in the car for a few minutes, remembering. We remembered people. We remembered the Wrens. We remembered the Neasons. We remembered the Thomases. Most of them are gone now – in Heaven. As we sat there in the car, our memories were filled with triumph and tragedy. On the one hand, those were days filled with wonder and awe and love and meaning and excitement. Great grace was upon us. We considered it our highest privilege to serve our Lord, the King of Kings, the Savior of our souls, the only sovereign and ruling God. On the other hand, we remembered the tribulations and hardships. I could, with the apostle Paul, name a few hardships.

Among the few was economic deprivation. Certainly as a graduate of Texas A&M University, I expected to get a nice job, and I did get a nice job. It just didn't pay very well. I think at the time we were getting about $100 a month for that one church, of the three churches we were charged with serving. In fact, I remember well one year when the Shiro church was considering salary increases. The song leader, who sang with a dip of tobacco in his mouth, said to me face-to-face, "You know, preacher, you're not worth the money we pay you, anyway!" That was his way of telling me I wasn't getting a raise.

Economic deprivation, emotional fatigue, and physical exhaustion. Why? Because we were also traveling back and forth to seminary at Perkins School of Theology, Southern

Methodist University, in Dallas. We went to Dallas during the week with our son, Jason, and our little black and white dog, Corky, in our little light blue Volkswagen bug. Here's our routine: We left Bedias at 10:00 on Sunday night, arrived in Dallas at 1:30 or 2:00 AM, studied, studied, studied during the week, and returned to Bedias, Iola, and Shiro on Fridays. We had services on Friday night, Saturday visitation of members that were ill or shut-in, services on Saturday night, and three services on Sunday. Sometimes on Sunday afternoon, we'd go to the nursing home. Then we packed back up for the drive back to Dallas on Sunday night. We were exhausted. We experienced soul bombardments, literal satanic attacks, sickness, auto accidents, and the like.

As we reflected there in front of that little church, a deep sense of satisfaction about this glorious life that God had given us filled our hearts, and we pondered, "How did we do it? How DID we do it?" Well, two things came to mind for sure: we were younger – thanks be to God – and we were naïve. We were just foolish enough to believe that this was it! This is what we were called to do – to spend our entire lives extravagantly serving God. We wondered how we survived it. How did we overcome the obstacles? Believe me, there were plenty. How did we rise up to face the challenges?

At first, Connie attributed our strength to our constitutions. She's got a stronger constitution than I do. She can outwork me any day, but when I was younger, I could almost keep up with her. She concluded that some people have a stronger constitution and work ethic than others. You just keep going when other people fall by the wayside. Strong constitution is in our DNA – the will to survive. You might say stamina. However, upon further reflection, we came to this conclusion. We said to each other, "Really, it was the grace and the power and perseverance and the fortitude granted to us by Almighty God, given to us primarily as a result of our faith." We knew then and we know now that it was God who created us for His purpose. It was God who called us to follow Him. It was our God who promised that He would never leave us nor forsake us. The secret to our rising up to face any and all challenges that we have faced along the way is our conviction that God is worthy of our ultimate allegiance. For us, there has been no nobler, more honorable or fulfilling privilege than serving the living God. At some point in our early adulthood, we became obsessed with knowing God, serving God, obeying God, and doing whatever God asked us to do, regardless of the hardships, the trials, and the challenges.

One of the keys, but not the only key, to our victory is our conviction that the Lord God Almighty has a purpose and a plan, and He has all the power we need to live victoriously. Oh, what a glorious life it has been, and still is by the grace of God! Let me put it in plain language: We think that for 41 years, it has not been just our will to survive, but it has been our absolutely solid constitution that says, "As for me and my house, we will serve the Lord" (Joshua 24:15).

That is the heart and the spirit of the apostle Paul in his letter to the Corinthians. Let me remind you what he says: "...we have this treasure in jars of clay," which is to say that we have this Gospel, this hope, this glorious relationship with God in us – the jars of clay. Why? "To show this all surpassing power is from God. We are hard pressed on every side, but not crushed; we are perplexed, but not in despair; we are persecuted, but not abandoned; we are struck down, but not destroyed." What was Paul's secret to facing the hardships, the difficulties, and the trials? Read verse 16 again. "Therefore (whenever you see "therefore" in the Bible, always ask yourself what the therefore is there for, because it always points to a conclusion) we do not lose heart." That is the issue. When you lose heart, you've lost everything! When you've lost heart, you haven't got much left to go on. So Paul says, "...we do not lose heart!" Why? "Though outwardly we are wasting away, yet inwardly (the heart) we are being renewed day by day. For our light and momentary troubles are achieving for us eternal glory that far outweighs them all." To put this into balance is to say that eternal glory (going to heaven) far outweighs any trouble or trial or hardships that I may face in serving Him. "So we fix our eyes not on what is seen, but on what is unseen, since what is seen is temporary, but what is unseen is eternal."

In Jim Collins' book *Good to Great,* he concludes this: "When all the pieces come together, not only does your work move toward greatness, but so does your life. For in the end, it is impossible to have a great life unless it is a meaningful life and it is very difficult to have a meaningful life without meaningful work. Perhaps then you might gain the tranquility that comes from knowing that you've had a part in creating something of intrinsic excellence that makes a contribution. Indeed, you might even gain the deepest of all satisfactions knowing that your short time here on this Earth has been well spent and that it mattered."

In the book *Breakout Churches*, Tom Rainer refers to this quote from Jim Collins and digs deeper when he says, "If making a difference in work is so meaningful, how much more meaningful is making a difference in God's work?" Got it? If meaningful work is valuable, how much more valuable does that work become when we work to make a difference in God's kingdom?

Here's the point: I believe that faith, belief, action, and conviction that God has a purpose and a plan for your life, along with believing in the nobility of honoring and serving the Master, will ignite your life with passion, courage, and fortitude. Listen, you have to get first things first in your life. If you want great grace and great strength and great courage and great purpose that gets you up and gets you going – facing every challenge in life with the will to survive and thrive – then give your entire life to serving Christ – who saves you, who forgives you, who heals you, who rescues you, who reconciles you, who loves you, and who changes you. He is worthy of your very best!

The New Testament is absolutely unmistakable, makes no apology, and leaves no shred of doubt about God's call in your life. God's call in your life is a call to radical love. It is a call for radical hospitality. It is a call to radical service. It is a call to extravagant devotion. It is a call to radical sacrifice. It is a call to holy living. It is a call to kingdom building. It is "Jesus first" living. Jesus made it clear: "Come follow me and I'll make you fishers of men" (Matthew 4:19). Jesus said in Luke 9:23, "Forsake everything and follow me. Take up your cross!" The apostle Paul made it clear that his one desire was "to know Christ and to make Him known." The apostle Peter made it clear. John Wesley made it clear. Where God's people down through the ages and the centuries have gotten that concept straight and clear in their hearts, and are completely immersed in Christ, they have transformed the world together. They don't have time or energy to waste on trivial matters of self-preservation, nor lackluster lives trapped in a maze of self-pity, apathy, lethargy, and boredom. You give yourself to something noble, something great, something beyond yourself, and you really grab hold of something worth living and worth dying for, and I guarantee you, God will meet you and give you whatever you need to traverse this life, so that you are able to meet the challenges you face. People who give themselves completely to the Lord are too busy rising up to meet the challenges of life to fix their attention on transient troubles. I'm talking about a passion that burns within. I'm talking about an unquenchable desire to serve the Lord, no matter what. I'm talking about a passion that says we'll get it done or we'll die. That's the kind of conviction and faith in action that will carry you through the challenges and carry you to the mountaintop.

Let's put it in plain language. If a mother says, "I'm going to forgo my privilege to be a stay-at-home mother by working and providing some economic advantage to our family for the sake of my children," that mother is willing to do just about anything for the sake of the call. She will endure hardships, because she's made a decision to do that. Tremendous energy and strength comes to you when you surrender in any area of your life, and you say, "I'm going to go for broke! I'm going to do it!" What I'm suggesting is that for the believer, there is no higher calling than doing it all for the glory of God. When you get that right, you don't have time to be preserving yourself and worrying about this or that. You're willing to press through and press on as you face the challenges of life. In the words of the writer (William P. Merrill, 1867-1954) of the great hymn, *Rise Up, O Men of God,* he pens:

> Rise up, O men of God
> Have done with lesser things
> Give heart and mind and soul and strength
> To serve the King of Kings

He will give you the grace and the strength and the courage and the hope and the tenacity that you need to rise above your obstacles and break through to your victory. Remember what Paul said: "Thanks be to God. He gives us the victory through our Lord Jesus Christ." So fix your eyes on the author of your faith – fix your eyes on Jesus, as Paul said. Not just what is seen, but what is unseen. What is unseen is eternal in the heavens, and therefore, you won't lose heart.

Now, Connie and I have been through some trials, and so have you. Undoubtedly we'll go through more trials, and so will you. But there is strength to face your trials when you really get gripped with the notion that you exist for the glory of God, and you want your life to bring God glory through your service and through your witness, no matter what you face. You will get the grace to go through it victoriously.

Right now, give your heart to serve Jesus, the King of Kings. God is faithful; He will never let you down. He will always pick you up.

Pray this prayer out loud:

Gracious and loving God, as I bow before the mystery of the Gospel of the good news, I hear the witness of our fathers who've gone before me and the saints who are with me, and I'm gripped, O God, with the nobleness, the grandness, and the greatness of serving you. God, forgive me that I have lost sight of that. Help me, Lord, regain my vision. Help me, Lord, to really get a hold deep down in my spirit, that any trials I go through pale in the light of this glorious good news – this Gospel of God's love – this great inheritance that is laid up for me. In Jesus' name. Amen.

It's What's Inside that Counts

"Thanks be to God. He gives us the victory through Jesus Christ our Lord." I Corinthians 15:57

Scripture Reading: I Corinthians 15:57, Genesis 37: 3, 4; 23-25, Luke 15:22-24

Key thought:

> In order to be victorious and to live your best life possible, you must see yourself the way God sees you – as unique, confident, hopeful, positive, gifted, capable, adequate, and secure. A healthy self-image is one of the key factors in rising up to meet the challenges of life!

Jacob loved his son, Joseph, profoundly. In fact, he loved him more than any of his other sons, because he had been born to him in his old age. To show Joseph how much he loved him, he made a richly ornamented robe for him. When his brothers saw that their father loved him more than any of them, they hated him and could not speak a kind word to him. Jealousy, like a cancer, grew in Joseph's brothers, until they plotted to kill Joseph by throwing him into a dry well and leaving him there to die. In their evil scheme to destroy him, they "stripped him of his robe – the richly ornamented robe he was wearing." The robe represented his father's love, favor, and honor. In effect, their actions were saying to Joseph: Who do you think you are? You are worthless. You are nobody, Joseph. Perhaps someone has questioned your worth by sarcastically, accusingly asking, *Who do you think you are?*

In the Bible, robes were always placed on people as a sign of their dignity, royalty, favor, and honor. To strip Joseph of his robe was a way of stripping him of his dignity, honor and favor. Although these brothers succeeded in stripping Joseph of his outer robe, they could not strip him of his inner belief that his father loved him. Joseph never lost confidence that his father favored him. How do I know? Joseph lived out the conviction that...IT'S WHAT WE BELIEVE ON THE INISDE THAT REALLY COUNTS.

Consider another son. The Prodigal Son collected his inheritance from his father and squandered his wealth on wild living. When he came home, his father ordered the servants to go quickly and bring "the best robe" and put it on him. He not only put the best robe on him, but also put a ring on his finger, and sandals on his feet. To celebrate his son's return home, his father ordered the fatted calf to be prepared for a party.

There is an interesting contrast between the Prodigal Son and Joseph. Joseph was stripped of his robe, but on the inside he never forgot his identity. He was greatly loved by his father, and so he lived his life with confidence, hope and integrity. Often in our own lives, people and circumstances attempt to strip us of our dignity and honor. Folks who have nothing kind to say about us victimize us. In contrast, the Prodigal Son surrendered his robe by his own choice. In other words, by his own actions, he caused the state of affairs that led to his loss of dignity. He demanded his inheritance, squandered it, and realized at some point that even his father's hired servants were treated better than he was treated. Then and only then, he returned home — not asking to be treated as a son, but only as a servant. What did his father do? He ordered his servants, "Bring the best robe for my son. Restore him to his place in our family."

Consider this! We can lose our dignity in one of two ways: 1) People strip us of our robe, or 2) we can make a mess of things all by ourselves, without anyone else's help. The good news is that ultimately, our Father God waits with a robe for every person.

In order to be a victorious, overcoming champion and to live your best life possible, you must see yourself the way God sees you – as a unique, confident, hopeful, positive, gifted, capable person. A healthy self-image is one of the key factors in living your best life possible, and rising up to meet the challenges of life.

Who do you think you are? That's the question God is asking you. Who do you think you are? The way you answer that question will determine a lot about the way you live your life. Joseph refused to be defeated. He knew that it's what's on the inside that counts. In spite of the fact that countless times in Joseph's life, people tried to strip him of his dignity, he kept holding on to his father's love; his father's confidence; his father's value; and Joseph believed in his inherent worth. In other words, he did not let somebody else's opinion determine his self-worth and value. He decided his worth based on his father's love.

In the July 2005 issue of *Reader's Digest*, there is a story about Kelley Sperry, a teenager with a very rare disease called Parry-Romberg Syndrome. Doctors began to detect it when Kelley was still in elementary school. Essentially what the disease does is destroy the skin, muscles, and bones in a person's face. As a young girl, the muscles in Kelley's face began to pull to one side. She looked like she had a mini-stroke. Because of the way she looked in elementary school, Kelley was teased and bullied unmercifully by her fellow students. They called her names like "crooked nose" or "Kelley face" or "funny face." Effectively, what all those kids were doing was stripping Kelley of her robe – her sense of well-being and self-esteem. Gradually, she began to shut everyone out of her life, even her parents. Kelley says, "I felt very bad about myself, and I never even wanted to look in the mirror." She remained unhappy and withdrawn as a child.

Her parents tried in every way to support her, protect her, and find answers for Kelley. They even went to her school to appeal to the teachers, to get the kids to back off their cruel, mean-spirited teasing. Finally, her parents decided to relocate and move to a new town. They made the right decision. In this new community, they found gracious, caring, loving people. The surrounding neighbors became their good friends, and when they discovered Kelley's disease, they treated her just like any normal child. They loved Kelley extravagantly. Kelley found new friends and became involved in school activities. Before long, she began to open up. Fourteen-year-old Breanne Graff became her best friend. When people asked Breanne about Kelley's face, she would tell them, "You shouldn't judge her by her appearance, because she has the coolest personality. She's a lot of fun to be around. No matter what, I stand up for her, because what hurts Kelley hurts me!"

Let me assure you today — if you have been hurt, whatever hurts you also hurts your heavenly Father.

Slowly but surely, Kelley made new friends. One day she realized that she was actually becoming popular. Now when Kelley is insulted for the way she looks, she says, "I shrug them off. I am comfortable with myself. If somebody else isn't, that's their problem." Kelley dreams of becoming a lawyer. She says, "I want to help people who are victims of crime or aren't being treated right. I think I'd be pretty good at that" (p.133). Although Kelley's symptoms continue to progress, and she will always look different from her friends, she is finding her way forward as an overcomer. The article's writer, Lisa Collier Cool, concludes, "Kelley has learned more profoundly than most kids her age – IT'S WHAT'S ON THE INSIDE THAT COUNTS."

Like Joseph of the Bible, and like Kelley, many of us have been stripped of our robes, our dignity, our worth, and our self-esteem. People and circumstances have robbed us of our belief in ourselves, that we are wanted, valuable, capable, gifted, likeable, and loveable. Our innate worth – the way we see ourselves – affects the way we speak and think and act and react in life.

Recently, while Connie and I were sitting on our back patio drinking coffee and enjoying the early morning sounds of chirping birds and chattering squirrels, she challenged me to write this book. She is always my champion. She wants me to reach my full potential and be my best person. She said, "You've got to write, Bruce. It's your next step. People need to have in their hands all the wonderful messages you have to share." I found myself resisting and withdrawing from the conversation. Through body language, I was saying, "I don't want to talk about it." She continued her monologue, and I became agitated. I began to make excuses about why I couldn't write – lame excuses that she quickly dispelled. Finally, she took my silence as the end of the conversation. In an agitated state of mind, I went upstairs to my study and wrote my feelings in my journal. The battle went like this:

> *Bruce, what hinders you from writing a book? Is it because you're not able to write?*
> *No!*
> *Is it because you don't have time to write?*
> *Well, that would be a good excuse.*

The more I wrote in my journal, the closer I came to the disturbing truth – my hindrance was internal. I wouldn't write the book because of self-doubt. Fear rose in me – the paralyzing thought that nobody would want to read what I write. That critical inner voice echoed, "You don't have anything important to say." The voice continued, "You can't do it." My challenge is to overcome the debilitating fear of failure and rejection. Then it came to me – the problem is not that I can't write. No, the problem is that I *believe* I can't write. My point is this: It's what's on the inside that counts the most.

Do you know how my robe of dignity, respect, honor, and confidence was taken? It was stripped from me in elementary school by teachers and others that had the authority to speak in my life. I developed a hidden belief that I'd better focus on my physical abilities instead of my intellectual abilities. So, I pursued athletics over reading, writing, and 'rithmetic. It's what's on the inside of you that determines your actions, your beliefs, your behaviors, and your accomplishments.

Many of you are held back because somewhere along the way, your robe has been stripped from you. It doesn't really help you to focus on the past. Like the Prodigal Son, it might have been your own doing, or like Joseph, it might have been circumstances out of your control. Many of you have been through horrible life experiences that are legitimate reasons why your dignity and intrinsic worth have been stripped from you. You know what? I'm rising up to meet the challenge, and you can too! Here's the point – if you think of yourself as unqualified, insignificant, unattractive, unwanted, inferior, incapable, and unworthy of love and acceptance – it will affect the way you live your life. You will act in accordance with your thoughts. On the other hand, if you have God's perspective, you will embrace confidence, achievement, determination, strength, and perseverance as your God-given inheritance. You will live your best life.

The good news is that you can change your self-image. If you suffer with self-doubt and low self-esteem, you can feel good about yourself. It's hard work. It's not an instant transformation, like a new paint job on an old, damaged car. It is a process of healing, reformation, forgiveness, a renewing of the mind, and behavior adjustments that take place over time. If you don't begin the journey, you will never get there. Believe me, it's worth the effort.

So, the first thing you need to do is start agreeing with God. He formed you with dignity and honor. He created you in His image. When God finished His creation of Adam and Eve, He declared, "It is very good" (Genesis 1:31). That's where God begins with you. You are valuable to God. You are wanted, loved, and cared for by God. You have gifts and graces and talents. God created you for a purpose. God sees you as essential in his plan. Unfortunately, we don't see ourselves as essential. We say things like, "I'm just a nobody." "What difference can I make?" "Why am I important?" Rather than focusing on your faults, your failures, and your imperfections, search God's word to find His truth. You will never see "the real you" that God sees until you start agreeing with God.

In addition to agreeing with God, the next step is to center on God instead of centering on your weaknesses. Anybody can point out his or her own faults, deficiencies, and imperfections – most of us do that quite well – but we need to focus on God's strength. God doesn't use perfect people. God uses ordinary people like you and me, faults and all, to do extraordinary things. Get rid of that "little man" syndrome. The "little man" syndrome operated in the twelve spies who went into the Promised Land to assess their potential new homeland. Ten brought back a mixed report to Moses, saying, "We went into the land to which you sent us, and it does flow with milk and honey! Here is its fruit. But the people who live there are powerful and the cities are fortified and very large...We can't attack those people...We seemed like grasshoppers in our own eyes" (Numbers 13:27, 31, 33). Only Joshua and Caleb focused on the greatness of God. They said, "If the Lord is pleased with us, he will lead us into the land and give it to us" (Numbers 14: 8). We've got to get rid of our "little man" mentality by focusing on God's strength and ability. Our God is a great and awesome God. With God, all things are possible!

Next, don't let people strip you of your robe! Avoid hanging around negative, doubtful, critical, judgmental, hopeless people. They will try to take your dignity and confidence from you. Remember this – it's what's on the inside of you that counts. They can take your robe, but they can't take your belief in your God-ordained worth. Don't surrender your confidence and belief that God created you with gifts, graces, and talents. You can be successful, and you can have the best life possible.

Start stepping out in faith. My good friend M. B. "Flip" Flippen says, "Change your behavior, and you will change your life." It's much easier to change your behavior than it is to change your feelings and thoughts. When you start changing your behaviors, your feelings will follow. Override your negative thinking that says, "I can't," and start acting on your dreams. Move out in faith. Speak up a little more in conversations, because you have something good to contribute. Start initiating and engaging in conversation with people. They need what you have to give. Set a goal to accomplish something, no matter how small, and step-by-step, inch-by-inch persevere until you accomplish your objective. It might take one or two or five years to accomplish your purpose, but get started now. You will get there. Beginning is half done! God is for you. He will help you. You can achieve what you can dream!

Who do you think you are? This is a personal question that God sets before you. In Joel Osteen's book *Your Best Life Now*, he tells a story about Carly. He says,

> ...By most standards Carly should not have made it. Overweight, with one leg slightly shorter than the other as the result of a childhood accident, Carly was the lone woman employed in a largely male-dominated field. She had to earn her right to be heard nearly every day. Some people laughed at her appearance or her halting walk; some made snide remarks behind her back, some were inconsiderate to her face, but Carly paid little attention. She knew

who she was and she knew she was good at what she did, so when other people attempted to put her down, she regarded them as having the problem. "Emotionally challenged," she often quipped about her detractors. Despite the factors working against her, Carly continued to receive one promotion after another, eventually becoming the CEO of her company and a highly sought after expert in her field. How did she do it? Carly's secret is her incredibly positive self-image. A devout Christian, Carly believes that she has been made in the image of God and that He gives her life intrinsic value. She doesn't strive for the approval of other people or depend on compliments from her superiors or peers to feel good about herself. Bright, friendly, articulate, and extremely competent at her work, Carly goes through life with a smile. While others shake their heads in amazement at her attitude, Carly is living her best life now!" (p. 55)

In order to be a victorious champion and live your best life possible, you must see yourself as a unique, confident, hopeful, gifted, wanted, valuable person. God wants you to accomplish great things, and here's what God wants to do for you. God wants to give you back your robe. Others have tried to strip you of your rightful robe – or you have stripped yourself. The robe symbolizes honor, dignity, royalty, value, favor, and blessing. God wants to put His best robe back on you. Like the Father of the Prodigal Son, God wants to put His robe of sonship on you. Like the Prodigal Son, we need to wake up, realize where we are, get out of our self-pity, and return to our heavenly Father who welcomes us home. He has a robe for everyone.

It doesn't matter what you have done. It doesn't matter what others have done to you. God loves you, and He celebrates you. God pushes past your shame, insecurity, and fear, greets you with a warm embrace, and throws his robe around your shoulders. My son – my daughter – I'm glad you are home. Let's have a party! Robes for you! Robes for everyone!

If you are aware that your dignity, your worth, and your value have been questioned; if you've been victimized by people, places and things; if there's an inner voice in you that calls out continuously – unworthy, unworthy, unworthy – then take a moment and allow God to restore your rightful place. Let Him, the One who created and loves you, return your robe – your best life possible.

How to Have Peace in Troubled Times

"Thanks be to God. He gives us the victory through Jesus Christ our Lord." I Corinthians 15:57

John 16:33

> 33 I have told you these things, so that in me you may have peace. In this world you will have trouble. But take heart! I have overcome the world.

There is a vintage gospel song entitled "Jesus is Coming Soon" (Winsett, R. E.), performed by the Oak Ridge Boys, which captures the heart of America today. Listen to these words:

> Troublesome times are here,
> Filling men's hearts with fear
> Freedom we all hold dear now is at stake
> Humbling your hearts to God
> Saves from the chastening rod
> Seek the way pilgrims trod, Christians awake...

Life is full of problems, isn't it, and there is no way to avoid problems or challenges or obstacles or crisis or disasters. In John 16:33, Jesus said to His grieving disciples, "In this world you will have trouble, but take heart, I have overcome the world." Notice that He didn't say you *might* have trouble, nor did He say you *could* have trouble. He said you *will* have trouble. So why are we so surprised when trouble comes along? The Lord promised it! Thanks be to God –

notice the note of victory in the second half of that verse, "...but take heart, I have overcome the world."

In this verse, there is a great contrast we often overlook. Jesus says at the beginning of this verse, "...in me you may have peace," but "...in this world you will have trouble." There is peace in Jesus, but there is trouble in the world. In other words, you will go through some troubles and some trials, as surely as you live, but in Me, Jesus says, you can still have peace.

So how do we have peace in troublesome times? I'd like to give you five suggestions. Suggestion number one: **release your grief**. The disciples in this text were beginning to grieve because Jesus was talking about His death. If you read the whole passage in John 16, Jesus is preparing them for His leaving them. The disciples were beginning to sense that the end was near, and He kept talking about "when I go away." Inevitably they asked what He meant by, "When I go away..." They questioned, *where is He going*? Jesus sensed their consternation about this, and He addresses their need to know by comparing their grief with the pain of a woman who gives birth to a child, but when the child is born into the world, her joy overcomes her pain. So He says, "I will see you again. Now is your time of grief, and then you will rejoice – no one can take your joy away."

Grief is a human emotion we feel when we experience any kind of loss – loss of a job or business, loss of our youth, loss of a home, loss in a relationship or friendship, loss of a limb, loss of a loved one. Maybe you have grief because you are a witness to a great tragedy of the magnitude of September 11. It could be that you still experience grief when you turn the TV on and hear about the families' lives that are absolutely destroyed because of terrorist activity in this world; there seems to be no end to it. Sometimes I just have to click it off, because I can't handle much more of this grief as I think about those families and what happened to them.

People feel all sorts of emotions when they grieve. When we face a crisis, we experience feelings of fear. We experience anger. We experience worry, depression, resentment, and helplessness. The most important thing for you to do when you experience the emotions of grief is to acknowledge those feelings to God. How can you find peace in troublesome times? You can say to yourself, as many Christians do: *You know, I shouldn't feel this way.* In other words, live in denial. But the better way to find peace is to tell God about it – to acknowledge those feelings before God, instead of stuffing them down and denying that these feelings exist.

God created us to feel emotions, which means we should feel them. We should own them, we should accept them, we should talk about them – and we ought to share them with someone else. Jesus said, "Blessed are those who mourn, for they will be comforted" (Matthew 5:4). So, how do you experience peace in troublesome times when you are filled with grief, like the disciples? You simply tell Jesus about your grief, and He will acknowledge your grief in the same manner that He did with His disciples. He comforted them by making a promise that they would see Him again. He told them, "No one can take your joy!" One way to put it is that we need to grieve well, or as one writer put it, we need to have "good grief." Good grief means you feel it, you own it, you experience it, you walk through it – you don't deny it. You express I'm angry, I'm hurt, I feel alone, I feel depressed, I feel a heaviness. I don't know that I can ever make it through this grievous experience. Jesus said, "For you shall be comforted."

Secondly, in order to have peace in troublesome times: **receive help from others**. Galatians 6:2 says, "Carry each other's burdens, and in this way, fulfill the law of Christ." We were not meant to walk through this life alone. We can receive help and grace from others as they walk beside us and help us carry our burdens. It is a huge mistake, when we're going through troublesome times, to isolate ourselves in the crisis. We all need the support, the presence, and the encouragement of other people, particularly in troublesome times. Don't isolate, but rather insulate yourself by surrounding yourself with supportive people. Let me make this appeal: as a pastor, I have walked with other people through a lot of troublesome times, too many to enumerate, but I have noticed something very dramatic. Those who are relationally connected to other believers (I can almost promise you!), will not walk alone. Somebody is going to come to their aid, to their side, and to their presence, and they do not have to walk alone.

Recently, while on a reunion vacation with my extended family, we noticed that our 4-year-old nephew's eyes were not tracking together. By the end of the third day, the left eye was obviously turned inward. We were concerned. When his mother returned home, she made an appointment with a pediatrician, who got little David in immediately. The pediatrician recommended making an appointment with an ophthalmologist. The ophthalmologist, concerned with the sudden onset of the symptoms, ordered an MRI. A malignant mass was discovered in his head. The CT scan showed that there were no further masses throughout his body. Almost immediately, loved ones and friends were contacted for prayer. Throughout the young parents' worst nightmare, they were insulated through the connection of friends and family. They did not have to face this crisis alone.

Those who are disconnected relationally walk alone, and when they go through troublesome times, they are isolated – there is just nobody there for them. It's a hard thing! I've done funerals with auditoriums full, and I've done graveside services where only one or two persons are there who even knew the person being buried. They had no one to walk with them. So, the appeal is that when you are going through troublesome times, the worst thing you can do is to isolate yourself. Insulate yourself – engage with others.

Don't only insulate yourself with others when you experience trouble, but connect with others before you get to troublesome times. You have to build relationships, make connections, and surround yourself with believers, so that when you go through troublesome times, you can receive help. If you have received help from others in troublesome times, you know the power of a person's presence. It is not even what they say when they are with you — it is just that they are there for you. Don't be afraid to reach out to people who are going through troublesome times, just because you don't know what to say. In fact, you might say the wrong thing anyway. Be brave enough to stand with them. Go to them – put your arm around them and say, "I don't know exactly what you are going through, but Jack, we're here for you." Wow! Connect by giving and receiving help from others in troublesome times.

Thirdly, to have peace in troublesome times: **choose to believe rather than to be bitter**. John 16:29-30 says:

> Then Jesus' disciples said, "Now you are speaking clearly and without figures of speech. [30]Now we can see that you know all things and that you do not even need to have anyone ask you questions. This makes us believe that you came from God."

Believe it or not, we all have the power to decide how tragedy and trouble affects our lives. If we choose bitterness, then we will only end up hurting ourselves, and it will shut the door on our own happiness. John Maxwell, in his book *Roadmap to Success*, says this: "You need to remember that what happens in you is more important than what happens to you." What happens in you is more important than what happens to you! You can control your attitude, but you have no control over the actions of others. You can choose what to put on your calendar, but you can't control today's circumstances. It is more important what happens in you, then what happens to you.

One skill that will help you make the choice to be better is to learn to focus on what's left, and not on what's lost. Remember, all is not lost. Make a list of all the good things in your life – a gratitude list. When you're going through troublesome times and you feel like you have no energy, no hope, and that all is lost, I recommend the practice of making a gratitude list.

I have a friend who was without work for months and months, and every time I would talk with him, the main focus of our conversations was his financial trouble arising from his inability to get a job. He placed application after application and couldn't get work. *Woe is me – everything is terrible!* I would exhort him to keep trying, keep going, keep looking for a job. Something is going to happen – the door is going to open. Lo and behold, after a long period of time, the door opened and he got a job. Wow! Wonderful! Several months later, he called me saying, "I hate this job. They make me work hard, they make me work long, and they don't pay me enough." I responded, "Hey! Weren't we talking a few months ago about how you didn't have a job? You need to make a gratitude list, brother! You need to get an attitude check here! You're just making yourself miserable complaining about your job."

Make a list of things for which you are grateful. You are grateful to God for what? What are you grateful to your friends and family for? As you make your gratitude list, you'll be amazed by the new spirit that will come over and into your heart. Picture what you are grateful for, list it, and talk to God about it. Complete this sentence to God: *Dear God, I'm grateful for...*

The more you express gratitude, the happier you will be, and the better you will feel. When I was a young student in an elementary science class, my teacher was trying to illustrate the difference that density makes in matter. I remember vividly that she filled up a beaker with water, and then she poured mercury into the water. As she continued pouring, the mercury displaced the water. The lesson was that things with more density displace things with less density.

My suggestion when you are going through troubled times is to add something into your mind and heart that has more density than the trouble you are going through. Make a gratitude list, and instead of focusing on your losses, focus on what you have left. The mercury of gratitude will displace the water of despair. Gratitude will change what you experience – what you're going through. It is impossible to be grateful and depressed at the same time.

Try this: smile and put your eyebrows down at the same time. Smiling opens our eyes. Now, lift your eyebrows and frown at the same time. It just doesn't work! Your face wasn't made that way, and the soul isn't made that way, either. You can't be depressed and bummed out and grateful at the same time.

A fourth way to have peace in troublesome times is to **clarify your real values**. Jesus said in Luke 12:15 that a man's life is not measured by how much he owns. A crisis helps clarify your values by showing you what really matters, and what really doesn't matter. We need to remember not to confuse our net worth with our self-worth. Jesus said don't confuse your possessions with your purpose in life. Don't confuse what you are living on with what you are living for. A tragedy, a crisis, and troublesome trials teach you that the most valuable things in the world aren't things. What matters most are relationships!

Recently, an interviewer of the victims of forest fires asked a man how he was going to cope with his house being destroyed. The man answered, "We've lost it all and we're sad, but we're still together as a family, and we're going to pull ourselves together and rebuild." For him, what he realized was most valuable was not his house, but his family. So focus on what you do have.

The fifth and final suggestion when you go through crisis or face a challenge: **it's time to rely on Christ.** Crisis has a way of moving us from our self-reliance to reliance on Christ. The apostle Paul said it this way in Philippians 4:12-13:

> I know what it is to be in need, and I know what it is to have plenty. I have learned the secret of being content in any and every situation, whether well fed

or hungry, whether living in plenty or in want. I can do all this through him who gives me strength.

When you go through troublesome times, remember that Jesus said you would have trouble in this life, but that you can have peace with God while you are going through trials. It's time to stand and pray. It's time to trust and obey. It's time to wait on the Lord and see what the Lord will do. It's time to believe that He will make a way where there seems to be no other way. Jesus told us these things so that in Him, we may have peace. Jesus said that He has overcome the world, so take heart. The inference in this passage is that if He overcame the world, then we can overcome the world, too! That's the inference! I have overcome the world, and because you live in Me, you can overcome every obstacle – every challenge that comes your way. You can be better and not bitter. You can be stronger. You can grow. There is still hope. Christ has a plan for your life!

I believe you can be victorious no matter what happens by doing these three things. First, lean on Christ for stability. Psalm 112 says:

> Blessed are those who fear the Lord, who find great delight in his commands. ²Their children will be mighty in the land; the generation of the upright will be blessed. ³Wealth and riches are in their houses, and their righteousness endures forever. ⁴Even in darkness light dawns for the upright, for those who are gracious and compassionate and righteous. ⁵Good will come to those who are generous and lend freely, who conduct their affairs with justice. ⁶Surely the righteous will never be shaken; they will be remembered forever. ⁷They will have no fear of bad news; their hearts are steadfast, trusting in the Lord.

Secondly, listen to Christ for directions. We should never get tired of claiming this promise in Jeremiah 29:11-13 (NIV):

> "¹¹For I know the plans I have for you," declares the Lord, "plans to prosper you and not to harm you, plans to give you hope and a future. ¹²Then you will call on me and come and pray to me, and I will listen to you. ¹³You will seek me and find me when you seek me with all your heart. ¹⁴ I will be found by you," declares the Lord, "and will bring you back from captivity. I will gather you from all the nations and places where I have banished you," declares the Lord, "and will bring you back to the place from which I carried you into exile."

Listen to Christ for directions. Christ still speaks to us, even in troublesome times. There's nothing like the whisper of the Holy Spirit in our hearts when we are going through troublesome times. His still small voice that will carry us, His guidance that will help us make sense, His presence that will give us courage. The Word of the Lord comes and gives us a lifeline to cling to.

Third, look to Christ for salvation. "Salvation is found," the Bible says in Acts 4:12, "in no one else, for there is no other name under heaven given to mankind by which we must be saved." I would like to broaden this idea of salvation. Salvation is more holistic, but we have narrowed it down to eternal life, or getting people ready for heaven. "Are you saved, brother?" is a question meant to determine whether you know that you are going to heaven when you die. God meant a whole lot more with the word salvation than merely getting people ready for heaven. In fact, more and more I'm coming to believe that what He was talking about was getting people ready for life – getting people ready for

Him. Salvation means healing. Salvation means provision. Salvation means being rescued. Salvation means freedom. Salvation means deliverance. The Greek word for salvation is "sozo," and it is a broader word. Salvation is found in no one else but Jesus Christ. The Lord helps us live our best life possible when we put our trust in Him. This means we can always have hope – we can live victoriously, we can live purposefully, we can live meaningfully in this life. We can live triumphantly, we can be overcomers, we can get up and live life the way God intended for us to live it when we put our trust in the Lord. We can live lovingly, we can live as a servant, we can live forgiving – we can have joy! Your best life possible begins with Jesus Christ. Rising up to meet the challenges – having peace in troublesome times – the first step begins with trusting Christ to save us.

You can take this step today – right now! Pray this prayer:

Dear God, I'm in troublesome times. I'm overwhelmed. I need a Savior who can help me make it through. I need a Savior who can lead me in the path of righteousness. I need you, Jesus, to come and take over my life. I need you, Jesus, to save me. I surrender to you, Jesus. I pray this in the name of Jesus Christ. Amen

How to Maintain Your Perspective When Life Doesn't Go the Way You Plan

"Thanks be to God. He gives us the victory through Jesus Christ our Lord." I Corinthians 15:57

I want you to know Christ – I'm inviting you to connect with Jesus Christ. I'm inviting you to come to a place in your spiritual life where you settle it with God – you make peace with God. You want to have peace with God, and God wants to have peace with you. He's made every provision for you to have peace with Him. You receive peace with God by surrendering to God and crying *uncle*– by saying, *God, I need You in my life, and I invite You into my life.* I can promise you this: Life will go better with Christ. It doesn't mean you will have a pain-free life or a trouble-free life. The Bible says that in this world, you will have tribulation, you will have troubles, you will have trials – but the good news is that we have victory through our Lord Jesus Christ. I believe there is enough grace and enough help and enough presence that God has for every one of us to rise above our struggles – to come through our pain. It doesn't always mean that whatever is happening goes away, but it means we get a different perspective. We get a heavenly perspective. We find the grace of God to move on in spite of what happens to us.

Another step in rising up to meet the challenges of life is to learn how to maintain your perspective when things don't go the way you planned. How often have you had things go wrong – not like you planned? I think there are some things we can learn and do to help us when things don't go exactly like we planned.

I'm a really fussy individual; just ask my wife, Connie. I am like the *princess and the pea!* She is much more easy-going with life. I tend to get all bent out of shape. I can feel every bump in the bed – I can make a mountain out of a molehill. I can turn things that seem like normal struggles into life-and-death issues. I can also make myself and everybody else around me sick with worry. How do we maintain perspective when things don't go exactly as we planned, or when terrible tragedy strikes?

Let me tell you about a man. In this man's life, all hell broke loose (you know what that means when all hell breaks loose). The man lost everything – literally everything: his livestock, his land, his home, and even his own children. Everything was stripped from him. Everything that could go wrong, did go wrong! It is often said, *if anything can go wrong – it will!* His livestock was raided by goat rustlers. A terrible storm with lightning flashes struck his herd of sheep. His camels were raided by neighboring tribes. And as if that weren't enough, a tornado struck his oldest son's home where he was hosting his brothers and sisters for dinner, and all of them were killed in this tornado. Finally, the man came down with a terrible disease, and his body was covered with sores –he had painful boils from head to toe. This poor man lost his property, his livelihood, his livestock, and his ten children. To lose only one child is horrific enough, and to lose two of your children is unspeakable. To lose ten children is unworldly, unbearable. On top of this, his wife, overwrought with sorrow, pain, grief, and loss, says to this poor man, "You know what – you ought to curse God and die."

Do you know who I am talking about? Job! I know you don't read Job for devotional reading on a regular basis, but I would submit to you that it's a good dose of reality, and a good dose of grace. As you read through it, you will discover that in fact a lot of songs we sing come right out of the Book of Job. I'll show you in a minute.

Job! How miserable can it get? As I read this book, I don't know anybody who's had it as hard as Job. I've known some horrible situations, but Job takes the cake! He really went through it, but in spite of all those tough times that Job went through, he had the courage and the strength and the grace and the will and the desire to continue living. He found in God the incredible grace to make sense out of terrible things that were happening in his life. Even though tragedy struck and terrible times came, he maintained his perspective. I submit to you that we all need a heavenly perspective when we go through troublesome times, in order to rise above the challenges of life.

Not long ago, I was feeling one those tragic moments in my life – a mountain out of a molehill. Life felt pretty heavy. I was lamenting my life and I was wringing my hands – I was feeling a lot of sadness. A good friend of mine sent me an email and said, "Listen, Bruce, we are going through troublesome times, but it's not a life-and-death matter. We will get through this." Then, he told me a story about a friend who was dying of cancer and struggling with real life and death issues – would he live or would he die? That's a life and death matter. So, I'm speaking to myself even as I write to you. Get perspective as you go through troublesome times.

Now Job had some friends – three friends to be exact. These three friends were well-meaning friends. They were buddies. Together they ran the community of faith, together they went to church, together they went to synagogue. They lived in community together – and they were probably reared together. These three friends allowed Job to grieve for one solid week, the Bible says. After the week was over and Job was still grieving, they came around with their reasons why Job was suffering. Each gave his perspective – these counselors of the body of Christ. We are going to help you understand why what you're going through is your fault. So, these dear friends offered their perspective for about 27 chapters of dialogue between themselves and Job. Putting it in a nutshell, here's the perspective these friends had for Job:

> Job, you messed up – you're a sinner. You aren't as righteous as you think you are, and what you're getting is exactly what you deserve! Somewhere in your life, along the way, you committed sins against God, and God is justified in his condemnation and His judgment. You are getting what you deserve. It's your fault – it's entirely your fault! The chastening you are receiving, you have brought upon yourself.

Doesn't this sound like something we say to each other? "You know, you're just reaping what you have sown," we say smugly to each other. Or somehow we insinuate that we're being punished by God. I cannot tell you how many times, as a pastor, I help people work through the tremendous shame and guilt they feel at the death of someone in their family or their life. They think: *It's my fault! God is punishing me – I'm getting what I deserve.* So, we come to the conclusion that we deserve what we get.

95

Part of the reason we come to that conclusion is because of the bad theology of our parents. Parents say to their children when they're little, "God is going to get you if you don't straighten up." Please don't say that to your children. Let's get parenting right! Just say:

> I'm going to punish you if you don't obey. I'm going to put you in time out, or I'm going to send you to your room.

The point is: don't put God in a negative place in a little child's mind. They are going to grow up believing that God is going to *get me*. Unfortunately, the church in various sectors fosters that kind of thinking: that God is going to get you. Let me say that certainly there may be a cause and effect when I do some dumb things that put me in a heap of trouble, and there are consequences for my behavior. Please know that not everything hard that happens to you is because you did something wrong. You live in this world, and Jesus said, "In this world you will have tribulation!" I'm human, I'm flesh, and things are going to happen. It's unexplainable – you can't reason your way through it, and you can't figure out why.

Job was wrestling with God. He was trying to figure this tragedy out, and his friends were trying to help him. So, while it may be true that we can bring a whole lot of suffering upon ourselves, it is not universally true. It should never be the sole basis of our perspective. What was Job's perspective, and what should we do when we go through tough times? These are four little nuggets that God has given me out of this story of Job.

Number one – this is the first perspective: Job did not sin against God when he was going through troublesome times.

Make up your mind now that when you go through troublesome times, you are not going to sin against God.

Job 1:20-22 (RSV)

> ²⁰ Then Job arose, and rent his robe, and shaved his head, and fell upon the ground, and worshiped. ²¹ And he said, "Naked I came from my mother's womb, and naked shall I return; the Lord gave, and the Lord has taken away; blessed be the name of the Lord." ²² In all this Job did not sin or charge God with wrong.

When you are going through troublesome times, resist sin; charging God with wrongdoing is synonymous with sin. Don't charge God with wrongdoing. A little further down in chapter 2 Job's wife says, "You should curse God and die." She said, "Do you still hold fast with integrity after knowing all that has happened to you – curse God and die." Job said, "You speak as one of the foolish women who speaks. Shall we indeed accept good from God and shall we not accept adversity." Commentary: In all of this, Job did not sin with his lips.

From a pastoral point of view and scripturally, we should be careful to not sin against God — not because it is all that bad, but because when you sin against God, you alienate yourself from God. You close your heart to God's leading. When you harden your heart and become full of rancor, and you have given a charge against God – blaming God, you're angry at God, sinning against God, withdrawn from God – you know who you hurt the worse? You don't hurt God. You know God is still God, whether you love Him or not. You hurt yourself! When we curse God, we close our hearts to the very God who will comfort and heal and restore us. When you sin against God, you are removing yourself from the place where God, who loves you, can heal you, give you perspective, and get you through this troublesome time.

What I see happening in Christians' lives is that we begin to sin against God in subtle ways: we pout, we withdraw, we go off in our little corner, and we say, *God doesn't care – nobody cares.* You know what? We end up alone. Winding up alone is not really fun. We hurt ourselves and probably hurt the people who love us and want to be there with us. So, when you go through tough times, this is the perspective – make up your mind that you will not sin against God. Say to yourself, *I will not sin against God!*

The second perspective from this story is in the same text: Job worshipped God when he went through this trial. See that? Job fell to the ground and worshipped and said, "Naked I came from my mother's womb, and naked shall I return; the Lord gave, and the Lord has taken away; blessed be the name of the Lord."

How could Job worship at a time like this? Let me tell you something. He wasn't at a praise service at Aldersgate on Sunday morning! I mean, this guy was hurting – he had lost everything, his children were dead. Listen carefully. He didn't know the end of the story at this point. The end of the story came, and after all was said and done, God gave him more children and more cattle and more land. You know what? Don't ever say this replaced those dead children; you cannot replace dead children! It doesn't replace them, but God gave him another chance – another life, more children, more land, more cattle, and Job forgave his friends in the end. If you go back to the beginning of the story, he didn't know the end of the story yet! He didn't know what the outcome would be, and yet it says he bowed down and ripped his robe – fell face down before God and worshipped Him.

It is easy to praise the Lord when everything is going great. The core value of our lives is that God is God, and we are not God! God is worthy to be worshipped, whether we predict the end of the story right or not. He's the Alpha and Omega, the beginning and the end, and I will trust God. Job worshipped God. What was Job's perspective?

> Naked I came from my mother's womb, and naked shall I return; the Lord gave, and the Lord has taken away; **blessed be the name of the Lord**.

What does this verse tell us about God? God is worthy of praise – no matter what! What was Job's perspective about God? God is sovereign. What is Job declaring about his faith in God? Trust! What else? God is Job's source – God is faithful. God has a destiny for Job's life. I see God's grace. How do I see grace? How do you come into this world? You come naked as a jaybird! *You ain't got nothing!* You know how you're going to go out – the same way you came in, with nothing! Anything you get between those two events is all good. For example: My mother births me, looks into my shiny, cooing face, and says, "I love you. Here's some milk. Here's a diaper. Here's a bed to sleep in." Praise God! It's all good – it's all a gift from God through my mom. I didn't bring anything in, and everything I get is from God through her.

When I go out, I will go out the same way. Job was making a profound statement of faith: naked came I – naked go I. The Lord gives – the Lord takes. Blessed be the name of the Lord! Job's perspective was that God is the sovereign ruler of his life. I may not understand it all – I may not even like it all – but I can and I will submit to God! Make up your mind now that when you go through troubled times, you will not sin against God by blaming God, and that you are going to worship God.

The third perspective is that Job questioned God about what was happening, but he never doubted. In Job 13:15, Job wrestles with God when he questions God, but he never abandons his commitment to God or his core values. Job concludes, "Though he slay me, yet, I will trust him. Even so, I will defend my own ways before him; he also shall be my salvation." It seems that Job is saying that God is God, and I don't really know a whole lot! The older you get, the more you know that you don't know a whole lot. The older you get, the less doctrinarian you become. The less finger-pointing and sure about the whole world you become.

So Job is saying, "Though he slay me, yet will I trust him, and even so, I will defend my own ways before Him." What does that sound like to you? I'm going to trust God, but I want to discuss it with you, God. Even so, He can do whatever He wants to with me, and I'm going to trust Him. Nonetheless, God, can we talk about this? Even so, I will defend myself before the Lord. It's okay to talk to God. It's okay to ask God. Let's break it open. It's safe to talk to God about these things that we don't understand.

In the church, we act like it's not okay to question. I think there's a difference between questioning God and wrestling with God; there are a lot of people in the Bible who wrestled with God. It goes all the way back to Genesis: Adam, Eve, Abraham, Moses, Noah, Joseph – they all wrestled with God. Jacob wrestled with God all night long, until God gave him a new name – Israel. Job reminds us, "Even so I would defend my own way before Him." Eventually, after God and I talk about it, I have to conclude: you're God and I am not.

I will praise You no matter what I face. And in the end, Job says that God also shall be my salvation.

Statements like this shake the very gates of Hell. Why? Nothing can stop the person who has made up his or her mind to fully commit to the Lord. God can have His way in that person's life. They will not be shaken. Listen, Christianity is going to make you suffer; you stick your neck out for Christ, and there are little sufferings that come along with that. Jesus is worthy of any suffering we experience. The Apostle Paul said of Christ in Hebrews 12:2, "For the joy set before him he endured the cross, scorning its shame, and sat down at the right hand of the throne of God." Christ experienced all that suffering on the cross to redeem a hurting humanity. No pain, no death, no hardship can separate us from the love of Christ, Paul says. When you go through tough times, it is okay to question, to reason, to wrestle – but in the end, never abandon your faith or your core values. If you do abandon them, you will end up on the rocks of despair and bitterness and become sour, angry, and unhappy. Look, it is miserable being on that side.

The third perspective: Job maintained an eternal perspective. Job 19:23-27 (RSV):

> 23 Oh that my words were written!
> Oh that they were inscribed in a book!
> 24 Oh that with an iron pen and lead
> they were graven in the rock forever!
> 25 For I know that my Redeemer lives,
> and at last he will stand upon the earth;
> 26 and after my skin has been thus destroyed,
> then from my flesh I shall see God,
> 27 whom I shall see on my side,
> and my eyes shall behold, and not another.

I know my Redeemer lives. Anything that happens in this life is not the end of the story. I know that because my Redeemer lives, someday on the last day He'll stand on the Earth, and I will see Him. There is life beyond the grave! Our key passage, First Corinthians chapter 15 verse 57, is set in this great description of heaven and resurrection and eternal life. "If in this life only you have hope," Paul said, "you of all people are most to be pitied. If Christ be not raised from the dead, you're still in your sins and trespasses" (1 Corinthians 15:19). So the resurrection, eternal life, and the hope of life after death is a promise, as sure and real as if we're standing here. There's a life beyond the grave; it's the ultimate hope! I'm getting ready for Heaven! Unlike Job's wife who told him to curse God and die, unlike his friends who told him none of this would have happened had he just lived a better life, Job saw beyond the here and the now to the eternal. I know my Redeemer lives!

I had a conversation with my precious little mom. She was about 80 at the time – her body was wearing out a little bit, parts beginning to break down. She has always been a very strong person, a very faithful person, a believer in Christ – a stalwart Christian lady. She sent an email telling us about her eye diseases. She has lost sight in one eye and the other eye was turning gray; she has macular degeneration. I think all you can do is try to keep macular degeneration from worsening; you can't really cure it. She confided in me, "Please pray for me – I'm really, really scared." For my mother to admit that she was scared meant she was really scared. So I called her, talked with her, and I asked her, "Mother, what are you scared about?" She said, "I'm afraid of needles – I don't like needles in the eye." While we were discussing the situation, she said, "But you know what, Son, Heaven is going to be even better than Earth. Heaven is not the last option – It's the best option!" It's not like ... well, just get through life and then go to Heaven when you die. No, her perspective is: Hey, when this life is over, I'm going to the best option. I'm going to get my crown of righteousness – I'm going to be with Jesus forever. I'm going to be in a place where the blind can see and the lame can walk. I can dance (She didn't say that, but she may find herself dancing in Heaven!). It's the best option! That's what Job is saying here – I know my Redeemer lives, and in the last days, though my skin is wilting away, I'm going to see my Lord!

Are you going through a trial right now in your life? I bet you are. In any given week, I will hear five or six stories of trials within our church family. Every kind of division and hurt in families – the loss of a child, animosity between family members – a lot of hearts hurt. When you go through tough times, think about maintaining your perspective. First, don't sin against God or harden your heart against God. He is your source of help and salvation and peace. You can find peace with God even when you go through a trial. Secondly, worship God as the sovereign ruler, the majestic creator. Third, never abandon your commitment to God. Fourth, maintain an eternal heavenly perspective.

I was reminded of this vintage song, *I'll Fly Away*, written by Alfred E. Brumley.

> Some glad morning when this life is o'er, I'll fly away
> To a home on God's celestial shore, I'll fly away.
> Refrain:
> I'll fly away, Oh Glory
> I'll fly away; (in the morning)

> When I die, Hallelujah, by and by,
> I'll fly away (I'll fly away).

Maintain your perspective when you go through troublesome times. You're going to fly away! It's not the last option; it's the best option! Which leads me to this: do you know that option in your life? Do you know for certain that you'll fly away? Have you received Christ into your heart? Have you trusted Jesus Christ with your life? Have you said to the Lord: Lord, I believe in You. I trust in You. Come into my life.

The Bible says in Romans 10:9-11 (NIV):

> [9] If you declare with your mouth, "Jesus is Lord," and believe in your heart that God raised him from the dead, you will be saved. [10] For it is with your heart that you believe and are justified, and it is with your mouth that you profess your faith and are saved. [11] As Scripture says, "Anyone who believes in him will never be put to shame."

We can know for certain. As I said in the beginning, I want to invite you, whoever you are, to put your trust in Jesus Christ – to get that heavenly perspective. You may be going through a tough time, but you can have peace with God. You may be going through a trial that is unspeakable, but you can have peace with God. Oh, you may feel like it's your fault – you're to blame. I knelt in front of a dear, precious church member sitting on her couch, took her face in my hands, and said, "It's not your fault. Your brother took his life because he was sad and couldn't find a way out. It's not your fault." She kept saying, "I could've done something. What did I do wrong?" Listen, you may be going through a horrendous time, but there's healing and grace for you in a relationship with Jesus Christ. You may have received the message all your life that it's your fault. God wants to come along you and say to you: I love you. I care about you. Can we be friends, forever?

If you want to connect with God through faith in Christ – to give your heart to Christ, find peace with God, and get an eternal perspective with God – you can do that right now. Simply pray this prayer:

Heavenly Father, I come to You now through the blood and in the name of Jesus Christ. Please forgive me for trying to run my own life. I turn my life over to You and ask that You come live in my heart and give me an eternal perspective. Give me a perspective that will last into eternity. I surrender my life to You. Thank You for forgiving me, cleansing me, and giving me Your peace. I accept Your free gift of eternal life. I am Yours and You are mine – forever – in Jesus' name. Amen.

Numbers 6:24-26 (RSV) – The Priestly Benediction

> 24 The LORD bless you and keep you:
> 25 The LORD make his face to shine upon you, and be gracious to you:
> 26 The LORD lift up his countenance upon you, and give you peace.

Hold On – Until – You Win Out

"Thanks be to God. He gives us the victory through Jesus Christ our Lord." I Corinthians 15:57

Scripture Reading: 1 Corinthians 15:57; Romans 5:1-5; James 1:1-4, 12

Key thought: You can meet the challenges of life by persevering through tough times. Perseverance helps you hold on until you win out!

You may be going through a tough time right now. You may be asking yourself – How am I going to make it? How can I hold on and keep going? How can I survive this holocaust? Where can I find help? The good news is that God has placed inside each of us an incredible will to survive, strength for the journey, and courage to face the toughest of times. If you are going through a trial, you do not have to stay in a trial. If you have been defeated, you do not have to stay defeated. If you are going through a difficult time in your life, you can overcome. There is enough grace and help from God to get you through this crisis in life. You have already come through some trials. You are a testimony of God's grace. You are living proof that God helps you get through. "Thanks be to God! He gives us victory through our Lord Jesus Christ!" (I Corinthians 15:57) Jesus said, "In this world you will have trouble, but take heart! I have overcome the world" (John 16:33). We will go through some hard times for sure, but I am so glad that faith in God is not just wishful thinking. It's strength for today, because we have Someone ready to help us.

In his book *Tough Times Don't Last, But Tough People Do*, Dr. Robert Schuller tells a story about surviving a frightful tornado the summer he spent with his father on their 160-acre farm in Iowa. It was a quiet June afternoon, and they were watching the storm clouds brewing from the vantage point of the front lawn, where they could see more than a mile across the rolling farmland. With alarming stillness, like a tiger crawling up on sleeping prey, the storm crept closer. Suddenly a black funnel cloud appeared in the dark sky. Mr. Schuller ordered the family to get into the car. They sped down the dirt road, fleeing for their lives. From a hill two miles away, they watched the wicked twister work its way through the countryside. As quickly as it had unleashed its fury, it lifted and disappeared – it was all over. The storm was gone.

Their lives were spared, but when they returned home to examine what had happened, they discovered that the tornado had ripped through their farm, destroying everything that they owned. As they sat in their car reeling from the scene, Dr. Schuller's dad pounded the steering wheel with his clenched fist and cried, "It's all gone, Jennie! Jennie, it's all gone! Twenty-six years, Jennie, and it's all gone in ten minutes" (P 28). Slowly Dr. Schuller's dad got out of the car, ordering everyone else to wait. He walked bit by bit through the rubble, wondering what to do, when he spotted a little plastic sign. That sign had hung on the wall above their dining room table. It simply said, "Keep Looking to Jesus." In that moment he sensed that this was a message from God. It echoed in his mind – Keep looking! Keep looking! The neighbors thought he was finished, but he was not finished, because he would not give up. He had holding-on power! Dr. Schuller writes in his book, "There is one ingredient that mountain moving faith, miracle generating faith, earthshaking faith, problem solving faith, and situation changing faith must have, and that ingredient is holding power"(P 28). Dr. Schuller's father held on, rebuilt their home, and overcame tough times, because he kept looking to Jesus.

You can hold on when you go through tough times, because God is holding on to you. Perseverance is the Bible's word for "holding on" faith. In the book of James 1:2-4, 12, we read:

> Consider it pure joy, my brothers, whenever you face trials of many kinds because you know the testing of your faith develops perseverance. Perseverance must finish its work so that we may be mature and complete, not lacking anything. Blessed is the man who perseveres under trial, because when he has stood the test, he will receive the crown of life that God has promised to those who love him.

The word "blessed" means "happy or to be envied." Do you want to be happy? Do you want the sweet satisfaction of knowing that others see strength in your life – that they envy your life? Persevere – keep going during troubled times. If you don't continue when times get tough, you won't be blessed. You could lose your place in the race of life by dropping out. Just think: You could be quitting just when the blessing was coming your way. You could be stopping just short of the prize – the real prize – "the crown of life that God has promised to those who love him." You must carry on under trial. Anyone can persevere during times of prosperity and success. That's easy to do! When everything is going great, the bills are paid, and you've got good health, it's effortless to persevere. We must be trained to persevere during trials if we are going to win the race of life.

Perseverance is the strength God gives you to keep going. It is the God-given ability to persist and strive in spite of your circumstances, your trials, your hardships. Even the will to survive is a gift from God. It is the endurance to run the race to the finish line. It is the difference between those who start, and those who finish. Perseverance is found in people who refuse to quit in the face of great discouragement. Remember, the Bible says, "Blessed is the man who perseveres under trial." Consider this – because you are persevering under trial, you are already blessed. There are God-given strategies that will help you cross the finish line.

The first thing to do is keep your eye on the prize! All athletes train to keep their eyes on the goal, the finish line. You need to have a goal, a purpose – a direction for your life. Trials, hardships and problems have a way of distracting us from our purpose and sidetracking us from our goals in life. They drain us of energy, strength, and joy. When we go through hard times, we become focused on the problems. Our goal becomes survival! God wants more than survival for us – he wants us to reach the goal of an abundant life! So get a good goal, a worthy perspective, and a great big idea that can only be accomplished with God's help, and then you will have all kinds of strength to keep going.

Connie and I have four beautiful children. Our goal from the beginning was to have a loving, hard-working, purpose driven, God-fearing, respectful, safe, secure and life-giving family. Our goal was to make it all the way through all the stages of life with our family intact. Were there obstacles, problems, hurdles, hardships, and troubles along the way? You bet there were, but we never gave up on our dream, no matter how tough things got. Our dream gave us energy, determination, strength, and courage. We're going to make it! When you are being tested by trials, take time to reassess your dreams and goals. Your strength will return when you focus on your goals and dreams, instead of being focused on the problems and survival. Dreams have the power to pull you forward. Get some goals, if you don't have any. Clarify what you intend to do. Write it down. Commit yourself to make it happen by the grace of God. Make it achievable.

The second thing to do is to get a winning perspective. The Apostle Paul's goal for his life could be summarized this way – to know Christ and to make Him known. Paul went through every conceivable trial: he was shipwrecked, beaten up, betrayed, stoned, and snake bit, yet he kept getting up! Life kept pushing him down, but he kept getting up. Why? He kept getting up because he wasn't finished knowing Christ and making Him known. His goal gave him holding-on strength.

To have that holding-on strength through trials, start taking responsibility for your choices. Stop complaining, grumbling, and griping. Stop making excuses. Stop blaming others, and start taking responsibility for your life. Stop FIXING THE BLAME and start FIXING THE PROBLEM!

A farmer's donkey fell into a well. The animal cried piteously for hours as the farmer tried to figure out what to do. Finally, he decided the animal was old and the well needed to be covered up anyway; it just wasn't worth it to retrieve the donkey. He invited all his neighbors to come over and help him. They all grabbed a shovel and started shoveling dirt into the well. At first the donkey realized what was happening and cried horribly. Then, to everyone's amazement, he quieted down. A few shovels later, the farmer looked down with astonishment at what he saw. With every shovel of dirt on his back, the donkey was doing something amazing. He would shake it off and take a step up. As the farmer's neighbors continued shoveling dirt on top of the animal, he would shake it off and take a step up. Pretty soon, everyone was amazed as the donkey stepped over the edge of the well and trotted off!

Life is going to shovel some dirt on you, all kinds of dirt. The trick to getting out of the well is to shake it off and take a step up. Each of our troubles is a stepping stone. We can get out of the deepest wells of life by not stopping and never giving up. SHAKE IT OFF AND TAKE A STEP UP!

Let me tell you a story – a story about a man who became a victor, rather than a victim. This man was Connie's father, my father-in-law, Ralph Waldo Plummer. As a 14-year-old boy, his life would forever be altered. One carefree afternoon while playing with a friend on a rope swing in the backyard, the unexpected happened. It was Ralph's turn to swing. Young Ralph distanced himself from the swing, ran for the rope, and with Herculean strength hoisted himself upward. Up and away he went, further than he had gone before – but this time his strength had betrayed him, because he had swung too high. Rather than falling back to the ground in a graceful arch, the rope snapped like a whip and cracked Ralph to the ground. Landing in the dirt on his right arm, he received a compound fracture (this means that the bone breaks through the skin). Rushed to the clinic, the doctor cleansed and set his broken arm, but within weeks a horrible smell emerged. His arm had become infected and developed gangrene, because penicillin had not yet been discovered. To save his life, the doctors amputated his arm above his elbow.

His mother, Verda Plummer, in her wisdom, insisted that he learn to take care of himself. She did not allow him to wallow in self-pity. She forced him to develop skills for survival and success. He learned to write with his left hand. He learned to tie his own shoes. He learned to dress himself, bathe himself, and function with one hand – and learn he did. He attended the University of Houston, became a Human Resources manager for Hughes Tools in Houston, and eventually established Plummer's Nursery and Landscape Company in Richmond, Texas. He literally built the nursery with his one leathery hand. With this determination, he became a successful businessman, the father of nine children, and a Christian leader who influenced hundreds for Jesus Christ. He was an amazing man. Rather than sit around and cry about what he had lost, he considered what he had left...his one hand, his sharp keen mind, his winsome personality, his hopes, his dreams, and his will to not only survive, but to thrive! Ralph Plummer did more with one arm than many a man with two arms.

You can either be a victim, or the victor. Absolutely nothing can stop you from doing what God has called you to do. Do not focus on what you have lost; instead, focus on what you have left! Begin identifying what you have. You have resources. You have others. You have gifts and skills and creativity. You have the Holy Spirit to embolden you and empower you. You have the amazing gospel – the good news to offer the world. You have a wonderful fellowship of people in your church who love God and care about you. You are loved by a great and awesome God. You have everything you need to be victorious. So rise up and face your challenge.

Additionally, you can hang on through the challenges of life by rejoicing – THERE IS POWER IN PRAISE! Paul tells us, "Rejoice in the hope of the glory of God" (Romans 5:2). The Psalmist announces that, "The heavens declare the glory of God" (Psalm 19:1) and continues with, "Ascribe to the Lord, glory and strength. Ascribe to the Lord the glory due his name!" (Psalm 29:1) The Bible is full of praise and honor and declaration of God's greatness. Get your mind fixed on the beauty of God, the character of God. The New Testament word for glory is *doxa*. This word, glory, is used to describe the nature, character and acts of God. (Vines, p 267) In other words, He embodies glory, and everything He does is glorious. Our God is an awesome God. Our hope is in this glorious God who is incomparable, indescribable, and loving. He is transcendent, above and yet imminent – he is near. He is immutable, unchanging. He is the same yesterday, today, and forever. God is creator, sovereign, ruler, prophet, priest and king. God's love, mercy, grace, and justice are beyond words. Put your hope in this glorious God, the Lord. Rejoice in the hope of the glory of God. Trust him, love him, honor him, praise him, worship him, and you will persevere through your trials.

My friend Frances gained strength to face her darkest hours by trusting in this glorious God. Hear Frances tell her story.

> What should have been the best years of my life became the dark night of my soul. I would be celebrating my 25th wedding anniversary, my sons

would both be in college, and at last my husband and I would experience a new phase of life. We were financially secure and had even joined the mid-life craze of yuppie Harley enthusiasts. We had a wonderful group of Christian friends with like circumstances who formed a loosely structured empty nest club – the Free Birds. Then, the "shoe dropped."

Suddenly, my last parent, my dear young mother, developed breast cancer and within months died. On our first visit to our youngest son's college campus, we received a distressing call from my brother-in-law saying that my husband's last parent, his mother, had a reoccurrence of cancer. She died within 72 hours. Three weeks later, we celebrated our 25th wedding anniversary with a barbeque and friends. Two weeks after that, my spouse returned to clean out his childhood home and attend his high school reunion. He came home with a cold distance between us, and shortly announced that he was not happy being married. He said he wanted out. I felt like someone had taken my heart and cut it out of my chest. How could this be? I thought I was dying. That day I wanted to get away – to just drive around aimlessly. As I stepped out the back door, there were two poinsettias sitting in my driveway, a reminder from a friend – from God – that I was not alone.

God showed up at every turn. It was the morning of the final court date. God was so good because both of my adult sons came home to be with me, neither fully aware that this was the day the divorce would be declared final. As a result of my son's flight being delayed, I had to move the court time back by a couple of hours. After getting my son settled at home, I made my way to the courthouse.

As I walked into the courtroom, I came upon an old friend who also was going through a divorce. What was the likelihood of crossing paths with an old friend at that time in that place in this city of millions? We comforted each other. It was the most surreal experience to stand before a stranger – the judge – and hear that my marriage of 25 years was dissolved. It was so cold! Am I here – is this me?

My friend asked to go to lunch, and although my stomach was in knots, I felt that God wanted me to go and care for her. The God of all comfort... I knew that God had prepared me to be part of His plan to console my friend, who was a young Christian. Imagine – I had just had the gavel laid to my marriage, and here I was encouraging someone else.

Later that afternoon, I felt an urge to be alone with God. I made my way to the sanctuary of my small church. I entered the dark, empty worship center. My soul was crying out to God – I, too, needed comfort. Approaching the wooden kneeling rail, my eyes centered on the cradled Bible on the altar table, and I sensed an inner nudge to read the opened page. Isaiah 54:5-7

> 5For your Maker is your husband—the LORD Almighty is his name— the Holy One of Israel is your Redeemer; he is called the God of all the earth. 6The LORD will call you back as if you were a wife deserted and distressed in spirit—a wife who married young, only to be

rejected," says your God. 7 "For a brief moment I abandoned you, but with deep compassion I will bring you back.

His presence filled the room, and I knew at that moment that I was not alone. I would live through this. I could rise up to meet this challenge.

Frances

You can hold on until you win out by praising your way through tough times. The Bible declares, "Consider it pure joy, my brothers, whenever you face trials of many kinds, because you know that the testing of your faith develops perseverance" (James 1:2, 3). "Be joyful always; pray continually; give thanks in all circumstances, for this is God's will for you in Christ Jesus" (I Thessalonians 5:16, 17, 18). The highest form of surrender and trust is praise. You can't praise God and resent God at the same time. When you get your heart full of praise and gratitude, your attitude, faith, energy, strength and courage will rise up. Praise opens our closed hearts and lifts our spirits beyond ourselves. That's why it's important to praise the Lord ANYHOW.

When we go through a hard time, we are focused on ourselves. "It's all about me!" "Look what those people did to me!" "Why is this happening to me?" "This isn't fair to me!" Every sentence ends with "me." When you get some praise in your heart, you will get "me" off your mind. Just as soon as you praise God in your toughest moments, you will have the courage to persevere and rise up to meet the challenge. You will have that holding-on faith.

Are you going through a tough time? This momentary setback will not last forever. You are going to make it. Keep your eyes on your goal. Take responsibility for your life. Remember, the scriptures say, "Thanks be to God! He gives us victory through our Lord Jesus Christ!" (I Corinthians 15:57) In addition, Jesus said, "In this world you will have trouble, but take heart! I have overcome the world" (John 16:33). Begin by getting on the right team – with the Captain, Lord Jesus, who has already overcome the world. Put your trust in Jesus. Give your life to Him, and He will give you the victory. Put your hope in the Lord and start praising your way through your problems. When you do that – when you accept the free gift of eternal life that Jesus offers – you can and you will HOLD ON UNTIL YOU WIN OUT!

Preparing Ahead for Times of Trouble

"Thanks be to God he gives us the victory through our Lord Jesus Christ." 1 Corinthians 15:57

1 Corinthians 9:24-27 (NIV)

> 24 Do you not know that in a race all the runners run, but only one gets the prize? Run in such a way as to get the prize. 25 Everyone who competes in the games goes into strict training. They do it to get a crown that will not last, but we do it to get a crown that will last forever. 26 Therefore I do not run like someone running aimlessly; I do not fight like a boxer beating the air. 27 No, I strike a blow to my body and make it my slave so that after I have preached to others, I myself will not be disqualified for the prize.

The main idea: It's too late to prepare for the challenges of life when you are going through the challenge. You've got to prepare ahead of time for the inevitable things that will happen in life.

It is inevitable that trials and tribulations and trouble and hardships are going to come our way. It is an inescapable reality of the human experience that the unforeseeable will happen — the unforgettable will happen. The things that we couldn't possibly imagine will happen. There is a principle that says if anything can go wrong, it will! You will face problems and difficulties and troubles, and you will have setbacks and hardships, but the good news is, "Thanks be to God. He gives us the victory through our Lord Jesus Christ." Through faith, we can overcome obstacles. We can rise above the tide of trouble, but we can't wait until we are thrown into the fiery furnace or into the lion's den to start getting ready. You have to get ready and be ready before the trial begins.

That's what I'm thinking about. You have to be ready for anything – all possible scenarios. Basically, what I want to share with you is how to prepare for the challenges of life. This thought came to me as I listened to the news talking about hurricanes. We track hurricanes long before they make landfall. There are preparations taking place. Nowadays, we have lots of technology that can predict where it will come in, with what intensity, the anticipated storm surge, the wind and rain and possible damage. Essentially, the purpose of the warning is to help us prepare for the storm's coming. As I watched, I thought, *this is a good parable for life.* There are storms that are going to come into your life. So we have to prepare – we have to train ourselves, we have to discipline ourselves in order to prepare for those storms in life. Prepare yourself, arm yourself, and discipline yourself for the storms of life.

As I pondered this more, my mind thought about soldiers who are asked to go and fight the enemy in a war. We take 18-year-old boys and girls, and in a two-year period of time or less, we train them and prepare them for battle. What are the essential things that we would give to them to prepare for battle? First, they need to get the PT right – physical training. Get in shape, boys and girls! They rise at 5:30 in the morning and hit the track to start developing physically, in order to prepare for battle. They have to maintain their physical training. Then they will be given some skill development. In addition, their officers will identify what jobs they are going to be doing, and the trainee will receive training for those jobs – skill development. Another area to be developed is mental discipline. Drill sergeants are noted for reducing the person to nothing, so that the drill sergeant can build the person back up for something greater. A person can't be only self-reliant, but must really understand what it means to be a person under authority, a person who takes orders, and a person who works with the team and the comrades. There is a routine to developing the mental discipline and character to produce in these kids courage, perseverance, endurance, comradeship, and loyalty — without which they cannot win the battle.

Consider professional athletes, too. They prepare to win the game. As Paul said, "If you are going to run, run to win." Again, there is the same process involved – physical training, skill development, mental training and character development, and practice, practice, practice. Musicians or artists or technicians, all are professionals and all require training. Remember when your children were little, you taught them to play baseball by sitting on the floor facing each other with your legs opened in a V shape, and you rolled the ball to them and they rolled it back to you? You gave them a nice, wide target area, and together you rolled the ball back and forth. When they got older, you might take a nice little ball and start to pitch it to them. You don't throw the hardball at them right away. You give them a soft pitch. You are teaching them eye-hand coordination.

When Jason was a little kid, because he was my firstborn, I was going to make an athlete out of him (He wasn't an athlete – he was a musician. Jordan, his younger brother, was the athlete.). I bought Jason his first glove; it was huge on his little hand. I had a hardball. I pitched it to him, and he didn't move the glove at all. The ball hit the glove and bounced right into his mouth. He said that he was finished – that's it, no more! Can we go play the piano or drums or something? This is no fun!

We begin in little, incremental steps to develop those skills in athletes. They don't get to be major league players without starting somewhere back in the beginning as a two- or three- or four- or 5-year-old working their way up in skill development, physical development, and character development.

My friend Lisa, an avid dog lover and trainer, shared this correlation of the obedience training of dogs and the Lord's training in our lives. She said:

> Actually, the systematic process of dog training is a lot like the way that the Lord progressively trains us for rising up in the trials of life and overcoming all obstacles. When I am teaching a novice dog the basic obedience exercises, I don't expect the beginner to be able to hold a sit-stay in the Walmart parking lot without first being able to do it in his living room, then his yard, and then a quiet park. When I'm first teaching him what "stay" means, I reward approximations of the behavior. Once he's getting the idea that "stay" means to keep his hind-end planted firmly on the ground, I fine-tune his behavior by rewarding only his best efforts. I shape the behavior so that his response to the command is immediate – when I give the command, the response is automatic.

When he understands what's expected of him, I proof him with distractions – I build experiences that will make him rock-solid in his execution of the command. I'll go to the end of the leash and tug lightly while reminding him to stay. He has to concentrate on doing his job – "I'm staying," sitting against my pull. We'll graduate to bigger distractions, like a ball rolling by, another dog walking nearby, a turtle meandering along, and whatever else I imagine. When trial day comes, we want his exercises to be precise, without hesitation, and rock-solid. No matter the distraction, whether there are kids hanging over the ring fence with hotdogs in their hands, or the wind is blowing, or there's a lot of noise from the grooming area, or something else unforeseen happens, we want our dogs solid on their training, focused, and ready for anything.

I recently witnessed a novice level obedience trial in which all the contestants were lined up, holding sit-stays with their backs to the ring fence. All of a sudden, a strong gust of wind from an approaching thunderstorm knocked the fencing down flat on the ground with a loud clatter. Of course, all the dogs looked over their shoulders to see what had happened, but all stayed exactly where they were. They trusted their owners to keep them safe, even though their owners were all the way across the ring from them and not standing right beside them at the moment. In the midst of a stressful event, they trusted their owners and they steadfastly stayed where they had been commanded to stay.

Police and military attack dogs are trained in a similar way. As young puppies, they are taught the fun game of biting and tugging on a burlap bag that is floating by and flapping enticingly from the hand of the decoy as he runs past. A little later, they learn the joy of grabbing a burlap bite sleeve designed specifically for puppies. As they grow, so does the intensity of the game! With my black Australian shepherd, when I was doing bite work I would reward a particularly desirable alligator-like grip by letting her take the item from me; we tussled for it, and when she latched on exceptionally well, I'd let her win by allowing her to take it from me. Being the game lover she was, though, she'd usually throw it right back to me so the game could continue!

As the adolescent dogs get more rock-solid in their running approach and bite, we add mild aversives like light stick hits from a split bamboo rod to their shoulders and heavily muscled sides of their backs. It's mostly noise, and it teaches them to persevere and win the sleeve, even if something disturbing is happening. Later, gunfire will be introduced. We want them to grab that sleeve and hang on and shake it, no matter what. We want them to believe they are invincible, so that on trial day when it's time for the courage test, they will charge with all the focus and intensity and desire they've got down the football field and take the fleeing decoy down. This is with gunfire and the "bad guy" overtly threatening them. That invincibility is built into them from day one. This is so that in a real street situation, when their human partner is in danger from an assailant with a gun or knife, the dog will not hesitate a microsecond, but will put all he's got into taking the thug down and immobilizing the arm holding the weapon. In so doing, he saves his officer's life. He and the officer work as a team; they are one.

Lisa McDonald

How do we prepare to face life's obstacles? I have three suggestions for you. First, we need to develop a sound doctrine and theology of God – develop a theology of faith in God. We need to develop a theology in God, not in our circumstances – in God, not in our feelings. We need to develop a portrait of God in our hearts of who God is and what God is like.

When do we start developing that kind of faith in children? We start in children's church. We start talking about what God is like, we tell Bible stories to them, and we hope that they are developing and growing a faith in God. The Bible is a book of faith about men and women who learned to trust in God. Faith in God is fundamental to making it through the challenges of life. If you don't have a sound theology of faith in God, you are probably going to end up emotionally bankrupt along the way.

What I mean is that a balanced view of the nature of God is so important to a victorious life. A lopsided view of God is that He is all loving and gives His children whatever they want. Thank goodness God doesn't give us everything we want. Nonetheless, God does give us everything we need. The other side – the side that balances this faith – is that God is not only a loving God, but He is a just God. There are two sides to God, love and justice. We need to develop an understanding of the mercy and grace of God. We need to develop a vision of God's sovereignty.

When I think about sovereignty, it means that He is king and I am not. The King can do whatever He wants to do, and He doesn't have to ask my permission. He doesn't answer to me and He doesn't consult with me. God is God, and God does what God wants to do, when God wants to do it, and the way God wants to do it. So, faith in the sovereignty of God, the glory of God, or the otherness of God means that God is the ruler of the universe, and that I can trust God. He can do what He wants to do, and that's got to be okay with me!

If it's not okay with me, then I'm going to have problems with God, and I won't have a faith that will carry me through those hard places in life. I want to appeal to you that when you read the Bible, read it not as a rule book, but as a relationship book. Read the Scriptures to know God, to know God's will, and God's ways – not to find your own self in the Bible. Go to the Bible to find God, and not to find your own self. When you find God, you will find yourself. Then, you'll find yourself safe in His arms.

Hebrews Chapter 11:1-2 (NIV) is this great litany of men and women in the Bible who learned to live by faith:

> [1] Now faith is confidence in what we hope for and assurance about what we do not see. [2] This is what the ancients were commended for.

They were commended that they lived their life by faith. Did they all get what they were aiming for? In fact he says that they didn't get everything they were aiming for, but they had a vision of the greatness of God, and the worthiness of God, the glory of God, and they lived to serve God. God didn't exist to serve them.

How does that help us rise up to meet the challenges of life? We develop faith muscles so that when trials come, we will not be crushed or perplexed. Somehow we'll find in the grace of God and in the person of God a way to not only experience that suffering or that hardship, but to find God in it, through it, and come out on the other side saying *God is God, He is still God and I love Him.* There are a lot of shipwrecked Christians in this world, and I believe they are shipwrecked because they are disappointed in God. How can you be disappointed in God? Only if you create a god who is not God. You create a god who is not the God of the Bible, and then you can be disappointed in that god. Remember, the first way to prepare for the hardships of life is to develop a sound understanding of faith in God.

The second step to preparing yourself is to align yourself with God's word. What this means is taking all the verbs of the Bible, whenever there's an action, and saying that's what God wants me to do. Aligning myself with God's word means that even though I'm going through a trial, God wants me to do what He says. There are plenty of examples of that in the Bible. For instance, Romans chapter 12 is full of verbs such as "love must be sincere" and "hate what is evil." Applying this in my life: What is the will of God? His will is to hate what is evil, and cling to what is good. What is the will of God when you are going through a trial? Find out what is good and cling to that – be devoted to one another in brotherly love, honor one another above yourselves, keep your spiritual fervor serving the Lord, be joyful in hope, patient in affliction, faithful in prayer. Share with God's people who are in need – practice hospitality. If you are going through a trial, your hardship doesn't mean you can stop doing those things and rationalize to yourself, *oops, wait, timeout, God!* No matter what you are going through, when you align yourself with God and God's word, He will carry you through.

Thirdly, develop character. Someone has said that talent is a gift, but character is a choice! We have no choice or control over a lot of things in life. We don't get to choose our parents or our upbringing, but we do choose our character. We create character each time we make a choice. Every time you choose to do the right thing, you grow stronger – that's character. Paul exhorts the Corinthian church when he says, "Run in such a way as to get the prize" (I Corinthians 9:24b). In other words, if you are going to run, run to win! Paul said that the prize for him was the upward and higher calling in Christ Jesus; that's the ultimate prize for Paul.

Even if you are going through a trial or struggle, run to win! I can see my high school football coach gathering us together in the locker room and saying, "Okay, you guys, you've been working out since August. You've been to two-a-day practices, you've learned your skills, those boys put on their pants the same way you put on your pants, and the question is: do you want it more than they want it? So let's suit up, get out there, and win this game!"

Paul is talking about the kind of spirit that has the determination to win. There is a spirit about your life that says: I'm going to win. I'm going to make it through. I'm going to be victorious. I'm going to overcome. I'm not going to be a victim. I'm not going to let circumstances dictate my life. I'm going to press through when the going gets tough.

Paul says also that everyone who competes in the game goes into strict training. Strict training requires discipline: disciplining the mind and doing spiritual training so that when challenges, hardships, and difficulties come, we are up for it. He goes on to say that athletes do it to get a crown that is perishing, but we do it to get a crown that will last forever.

Then he says to persevere: "I beat my body and make it my slave" (I Corinthians 9:27). This is an interesting phrase meaning that your body must be your slave, and not the other way around. You're not to be dictated to by your body or your circumstances, but you are to dictate the way things are to go in your life. I beat my body and make it my slave, so that I myself will not be disqualified. Perseverance, training, and discipline – run so you get the prize.

Don't wait for the trials to come to you; get ready for the trials ahead of time. Prepare yourself for victory. Develop the spiritual muscles of faith, obedience, and trust. So that even when you are going through hard times, you won't quit; you are going to keep going. You are going to keep believing, and find a way forward. Submit yourself to God. Center your life in God's purposes and prepare for the inevitable – you will face trial. Jesus promised, "In this world you will have trouble, but I have overcome the world" (John 16:33).

I do not want to leave this on the note that this is all up to me. If this is all up to me, I'm in trouble! That becomes very man-centered and relegates the focus to what I can do to achieve. Most of us know that we can achieve very little without the Lord. There is a partnership between what God does and what we do. There is a certain sense in which we say that it all depends on God, and yet that is not the whole picture. The outcome also depends on us, and on our choices and our decisions. Without the grace of God, we won't make those choices and those decisions. God is the redeeming God, and God will help you through whatever trial you face. God will make a way.

There are so many stories in the Bible that illustrate this. One that comes to my mind is found in Exodus 15, when the Israelites were going through the wilderness. They had crossed the Red Sea, and the first thing they got to was bitter water unfit to drink. They began to complain against God because of the bitter water. God, in spite of their complaining, supplied sweet water for them to drink. If that wasn't enough, as they got further into the wilderness and became disgruntled about the food that they were eating, God, in spite of their complaining, gave them fresh manna every day and fresh meat every day to eat. In spite of the fact that they were wandering in the wilderness because of their disobedience, He still didn't let the soles of their shoes wear out. He preserved them in that wilderness. This shows that in spite of the fact that we are sinners and we have blown it in our lives, Jesus still offers every one of us the grace that we need to be forgiven, and to change our lives and change our hearts.

Continuously prepare! When we talk about the second coming of Christ, I cannot figure it all out. How, when and who – that's for God to decide, but I do believe this with all my heart, that there is an end of time. There is a great day of reckoning coming. There is a day of judgment coming. There is a day when we will realize *that time is not on our side*. Time is over – the whistle has been blown. When you get over into Matthew 24, Jesus talks about the coming of the Lord, and His emphasis is all about preparation. It's all about readiness. It's all about being ready. You remember the story from Matthew 25 about the ten virgins. Five had plenty of oil in their lamps, and while they were waiting for the bridegroom to join the feast, the other five ran out of oil and their lamps burned out. The five ill-fated virgins left to find more oil, and when the bridegroom came, they were nowhere to be found; they were left behind. The virgins who had prepared with plenty of oil were ready when the bridegroom came. He called to His bride, and away they went.

The ultimate question is: are you ready to meet the Lord? Have you prepared yourself to meet the Lord? We sing, *"Jesus is coming soon."* That has been the cry of the church for 2,000 years, but do you know what? It may be tomorrow. It may be tonight. Are you ready? Are you ready to meet your Maker? Do you have peace with God? Have you made peace with God? While you get ready to meet Him, have you prepared for the ultimate trip?

How would you prepare to make peace with God and to be ready? Essentially and fundamentally, it is this – Romans chapter 10 says, "If you believe in your heart that God raised Jesus Christ from the dead and you confess with your mouth that Jesus is Lord you will be saved." Those are the two conditions – believe in your heart and confess with your mouth that Jesus Christ is Lord; you will be saved. You can be born again. You can be ready. You can be ready to meet your Maker, and you can even reach the place where you anticipate His coming and say in your heart, *"Maranatha! Even so, come Lord Jesus; I'm ready for You."*

Have you made your preparations? Do you know for certain that you will be ready to go when He calls your name? Have you made peace with God? Pray this prayer:

Lord, even if I haven't prepared properly for the trials of life, I ask for Your mercy and grace. I ask You, Lord, that in the trials I am going through, whether it be a financial trial, a health issue trial, a relationship trial, or an addiction trial I am facing today, even if I feel crushed by those trials, I ask You for mercy. Please deliver me through this trial and use this trial as a training ground for the next one. I pray that this trial will not be wasted or lost in preparing me to be strong in the Lord, and to persevere in trial, and know that the Lord is the Lord of Heaven and Earth.

Lord, I ask for Your blessing and favor as I go through this trial. Lord, I pray that like runners, athletes, and soldiers, that I will have sense enough to get ready for the next trial. Lord, I will not wait until I'm in it; I will develop my faith muscles by reading Your word, worshiping, fellowshipping, talking about You and to You, learning about You, and learning Your ways, Lord. Make me pliable and mold me into Your image, Lord Jesus, so that when I go into the trials, I will be like Daniel; I will be able to face the lion's den. Throw me in the lion's den; my God is able to deliver me. Shadrach, Meshach, and Abednego would not compromise their faith. They were thrown into the fiery furnace. Even the ones who threw them into the fiery furnace were consumed by the fire, but those three faithful followers of the Living God were not consumed! Lord, I pray that I will grow in my faith muscles, so that I will not be consumed in the fiery furnace of life. Lord, give me a hunger for You, a determination to win, a determination to be victorious, and to walk in the victory that You have provide.

Lord, I pray that today is my day. I want be right with You, O God. I want to know Christ and have peace with God. Please forgive me and make me ready. I want to live life well. This I pray in the name of Jesus. Amen.

Works Cited

Biblica, Inc. *Holy Bible, New International Version, NIV.* Biblica, Inc., 1973, 1978, 1984, 2011.

Collins, James C. *Good to Great.* William Collins, 2001.

Cool, Lisa Collier. *Reader's Digest* July 2005: 133.

Flippen, Flip. *The Flip Side.* New York, NY: Springboard Press, 2007.

Maxwell, John C. *Thinking for Change.* New York, New York: Warner Books, Inc., 2003.

—. *Your Road Map for Success.* A Georgia Corporation: Maxwell Motivation, Inc., 2002.

Merrill, William P. "Rise Up, O Men of God." 1867-1954.

Osteen, Joel. *Your Best Life Now.* New York, New York: Hachette Book Group USA, 2007.

Phillips, Craig, & Dean. "I Am a Friend of God." 2000.

Pitts, William S and Randy Owen. "Church In The Wildwood." n.d.

Rainer, Tom. *Breakout Churches.* Grand Rapids, Michigan: Zondervan, 2005.

Schuller, Robert. *Tough Times Never Last, But Tough People Do!* Nashville, Tennesee 37214: Thomas Nelson, Inc., 1983.

Survivor. "Eye of the Tiger." *Eye of the Tiger.* By James Michael Peterik, Jim Peterik Frank Sullivan. 1982.

Vine, W. E., Merrill F. Unger, William White, Jr. *Vine's Expository Dictionary of Biblical Words.* Nashville, Camden, New York: Thomas Nelson Publishers, 1985.

Vujicic, Nick. *http://www.lifewithoutlimbs.org/about-nick/bio/.* n.d. Web site. 12 August 2014.

Warren, Rick. *The Purpose Driven Life.* Grand Rapids, Michigan: Zondervan, 2002.